Sovereign Sister

She Who Owns HerSelf

By
Rev. E.M. Whitefeather

SOVEREIGN SISTER

She Who Owns HerSelf

DEDICATION

To All My Sisters...

May We Be the Ones We Have Been Waiting For.... This is our now moment...feel the call of your Spirit...the fire stirring in your heart and the quickening of your Breath. Now is the time we must unite in our quest, our prayer and our destiny toward Sovereignty. Our liberation is the liberation for the next generations. It is the resurrection of Love and Compassion that can transform our world and reclaim our Dream of a more just, equitable, and thriving society where we All can thrive; and where we All can contribute to a world, we all deserve to live in-FREE from fear and the intimidation and oppression of the antiquated Patriarchy, whose time is now ending. It is time to place all of the darkness on "The Altar of the Done" and create within the empty Medicine Bowl the vision of our future the world our grandmothers have held in Sacred Space for 2000 years. Sovereign Sister, it is time to own your whole Self! Sovereign Sisters, it is time to reclaim and restore our innate power!

Blessings, Elaine

CONTENTS

INTRODUCTION

We live in a time of transformative potential. Across the globe, women and those identifying as female are awakening to their inherent power and are challenging the long-standing structures that have limited their autonomy. This book is an ode to this awakening. It's a rallying cry, a guide, and a source of inspiration for every woman who feels the stirrings of change in her heart. Together, we'll explore the path to reclaiming our body, mind, heart, and spirit from the clutches of patriarchy.

The journey of reclaiming one's autonomy isn't new, yet it feels more urgent than ever. Oppression, in its many forms, has historically sought to silence, marginalize, and control women. However, throughout history, women have also stood firm, fought back, and triumphed. This book delves into that rich history to draw lessons and strength. It's about honoring our past while fervently looking towards a future where our sovereignty isn't questioned but celebrated.

Empowerment doesn't happen in isolation. It exists in the quiet moments of self-awareness and the thunderous roars of collective action. Throughout this book, we'll explore how every woman's individual journey of reclaiming her autonomy can contribute to a larger tapestry of global change. It's a tapestry woven with threads of resilience, wisdom, and unwavering sisterhood.

To begin reclaiming our autonomy requires recognizing where it's been taken from us. This means addressing the subtle and overt ways patriarchy affects our lives: from societal expectations and cultural norms to the internalized beliefs that limit our potential. By unearthing these influences, we gain the clarity to redefine our identity on our terms, free from external impositions.

The stakes are high, but so is our potential. Each chapter in this book serves as a steppingstone towards not just understanding our power but harnessing it. In "The Winds of Change are Here," we'll examine the shifting paradigm that's allowing women to reclaim their sovereignty and the global historical context that has shaped our current struggles.

We'll scrutinize the forces that have maintained the patriarchal status quo. Understanding "The Goal of the Patriarchal Paradigm" helps us recognize the shadow strategy of power, control, and privilege that perpetuates inequality. Knowing the impact of these forces isn't about dwelling on the negatives but recognizing the challenges we must overcome to succeed.

Past resistance efforts hold invaluable lessons. In "Old Ways of Resistance to Oppression," we'll explore victories and subsequent patriarchal reactions, revealing the wisdom gained from these efforts. Understanding our true power and recognizing the potential within each of us serves as a bedrock for future triumphs.

"The Liberation of Your Whole Self" focuses on the personal journey, encouraging you to own every part of your being. Confronting where you're not free and understanding you're not your trauma are essential steps towards genuine liberation. This section offers a roadmap for reclaiming your identity and choosing who you are, independent of past struggles.

Transformation emerges from embracing both the painful and powerful parts of our story. In "Transforming Trauma into Power," we acknowledge the pain but also recognize the strengths gained in survival. Catalyzing these strengths can fuel a profound sense of purpose, propelling us forward with renewed vigor and clarity.

Healing is not just individual but communal. "Healing Sisterhood Wounds" addresses internalized patriarchal beliefs and the harm we sometimes cause within our sisterhood. By healing these wounds, we strengthen our collective ability to drive meaningful change. It's about fostering a sisterhood built on understanding, compassion, and shared resilience.

Our journey is guided by those who have walked the path before us. "WayShowers and Truthtellers" introduces compassionate leaders who lead with heart and vulnerability. Learning from their journeys helps us own our voice and understand that truth lives in the heart.

Visionaries and wisdom keepers remind us that we're part of a continuum that stretches back to our ancestors and forward to future generations. "The Dream Makers and WisdomKeepers" highlight the significance of using past experiences to shape tomorrow's dreams. Embracing ancestral wisdom ensures that the knowledge and values we hold dear continue to flourish.

A sovereign sisterhood is built on principles of equality, unity, and reverence for one another and our Earth Mother. "Principles of a Sovereign Sisterhood" delves into these foundational values, emphasizing how each woman's life is sacred and interconnected with the greater whole.

The journey of empowerment includes passing down these values to future leaders. "Empowering the Next Generation" focuses on teaching sovereign principles and nurturing leadership qualities in tomorrow's changemakers. It's about ensuring the torch of autonomy and empowerment continues to light the way for generations to come.

Ultimately, knowledge without action is inert. "Inspiring Action" urges us to mobilize for change now. Collective efforts and movements are the lifeblood of sustainable transformation. By the end of this book, you'll be equipped not just with understanding but with actionable steps to contribute to the collective liberation of women worldwide.

As we embark on this journey together, remember that you hold immense power within you. This book is your companion, offering guidance, inspiration, and practical steps to reclaim your autonomy. Let's dare to dream, to heal, and to transform. The road ahead may be challenging, but it's paved with possibilities. Welcome to the start of our shared journey towards a sovereign sisterhood, where every woman's power is recognized, celebrated, and unleashed.

CHAPTER 1:
THE WINDS OF CHANGE ARE HERE

A quiet revolution is brewing, and it's one that can't be ignored any longer. The winds of change have arrived, bringing with them an undeniable energy, an electric charge that whispers of transformation and liberation. It's time for women everywhere to reclaim what has always been theirs: their autonomy, their voice, their essence. No longer will we be silent or sit on the sidelines of our own lives.

For centuries, women have been conditioned to accept a lesser role, to bow to the patriarchal structures that have defined and confined them. This framework is not just historical; it permeates our present, creeping into our workplaces, our households, even our self-conceptions. But there is a resilience in women, a force that can move mountains. When one of us rises, it lights a spark in countless others. That spark has now become a blazing fire, impossible to extinguish.

The paradigm is shifting. Everywhere you look, women are stepping into their power, questioning the status quo, and demanding their rightful place at the table. This isn't just about breaking glass ceilings; it's about smashing the entire glasshouse and reconstructing it from the ground up, stronger and more inclusive than ever before.

It's essential to recognize that this transformation is not a monolithic movement. It's a tapestry woven from countless threads, each one unique but interconnected. The struggles of women around the world, regardless of background, are intricately linked. When we celebrate a victory for one, we galvanize hope for many. These winds of change are here to break down barriers, not just in societal roles and expectations-but within ourselves.

This journey will require us to confront uncomfortable truths and to dismantle deeply ingrained beliefs about our capabilities and place in the world. But it also offers the exhilarating promise of discovery—of our strength, our purpose, and our boundless potential to enact change.

So, as the winds of change howl and beckon, let us not merely stand by and watch. Let us join hands, raise our voices, and march forward with courage and conviction. The time for change is not tomorrow; it is now. And it is up to us—to you, to me, to each of us—to seize this moment and transform it into a dawn of true empowerment.

A Paradigm Shift in Women's Sovereignty

As the winds of change blow through our societies, a transformative shift in women's sovereignty is unmistakable. This shift isn't just perceived—it is felt deeply, in the marrow of our collective bones. No longer are we content to live under the constraints that have stifled our potential for centuries. We are reclaiming our place in this world with the full force of our intelligence, compassion, and indomitable spirit.

Change begins within. Autonomy starts when we recognize our intrinsic power. For many women, this awakening is revolutionary. It's the spark that sets everything else in motion. We understand that our roles aren't defined by patriarchal structures but by our limitless potential. When we claim sovereignty over our lives, we're not only changing our personal narratives but also rewriting the larger story of what it means to be a woman in today's world.

This paradigm shift is not merely an individual journey—it's a collective charge. We are more connected than ever, by shared experiences and through communities that span continents. The movements that have arisen recently—from #MeToo to global feminist mobilizations—demonstrate the power of collective action. The voices that have been silenced for too long are finally being heard, and there is no turning back. We must push forward with unrelenting determination.

Her sovereignty includes the reclamation of every aspect of her Being: body, mind, heart, and spirit. Our autonomy over our bodies is fundamental, but it extends further. Claiming sovereignty over our minds empowers us with the freedom to think critically, to question, and to innovate. Owning our hearts allows us to nurture our emotional intelligence and create empathetic connections with others. Embracing our spiritual selves opens doors to deeper understandings of faith, purpose, and the interconnectedness of all life.

The paradigm shift isn't just about breaking free from oppressive structures; it's about constructing a new world where women are cherished and celebrated. This new paradigm values collaboration over competition, compassion over dominance, and unity over division. It's a paradigm where each woman's sovereignty is honored, where her voice is not just heard but amplified.

In navigating this shift, we are inspired by the resilience and wisdom of those who came before us. Historical figures and everyday heroines alike have paved the way, and their legacies fuel our journey. As we honor their struggles and triumphs, we understand that our current liberation efforts are part of a long continuum. This awareness grounds us and strengthens our resolve.

It requires courage to move against the current and claim what's rightfully ours. Yet, courage is something women have in abundance. Every day, in countless ways—both grand and subtle—we demonstrate our bravery and resilience. Whether by leading organizations, nurturing families, engaging in activism, or simply asserting our right to be, we prove that the feminine spirit is a powerful force of change.

These winds of change are a clarion call to each of us to rise up and embrace our sovereignty. This call is both a privilege and a responsibility. As we answer it, we not only transform our own lives but also create ripples that will impact future generations. By embodying the principles of this new paradigm, we set the stage for a world where our daughters, nieces, and granddaughters can flourish in their full potential, free from the shackles of antiquated paradigms.

This is our moment. The shift is happening now, and we are the architects of this brave new world. As we continue on this path, let us remember that we're not alone—our sisters walk beside us, their hands intertwined with ours, their hearts beating in unison with the rhythm of change. Together, we will achieve the sovereignty that has always been our birthright.

Global Historical Paradigm of Oppression

The story of women's oppression is a tale as old as time, lodged deeply in the annals of human history. Across cultures and continents, the narrative has been remarkably similar: systems designed to hold women back, to keep them from realizing their full potential. This paradigm has persisted not because it is just, but because it has been deeply ingrained in the very fabric of society. But understanding this history is critical. It provides a key to decipher the mechanisms of control and to dismantle them piece by piece.

One must look no further than ancient civilizations to witness the roots of this systemic oppression. In many early societies, women were often considered property, their roles confined to the domestic sphere. They were deprived of education, political voice, and economic opportunities. Patriarchal societies like those in Ancient Greece and Rome relegated women to secondary status, using religion, tradition, and even law to justify their exclusion. These constraints not only limited women's lives but also deprived humanity of the full wealth of their contributions.

Throughout history, the oppression of women has taken many forms, evolving in complexity and cruelty. The Middle Ages saw the rise of witch hunts that targeted women who dared to defy societal norms or who simply happened to be in the wrong place at the wrong time. These persecutions were often thinly veiled attempts to control women's power and autonomy. By labeling women as witches, society could justify their execution and subjugation, thereby maintaining the existing power dynamics. The echoes of these injustices still resonate today, reminding us of the cyclical nature of oppression.

During the Industrial Revolution, the picture shifted again. Women entered the workforce, but their experiences were far from liberating. They found themselves in grueling conditions, working long hours for meager pay. The factories exploited their labor while offering little in return—no rights, no benefits, and no respect. Yet this period also sparked the earliest waves of feminist consciousness, as women began to unite, demanding fair wages and better working conditions. These early struggles laid the groundwork for the suffrage movements and the broader quest for women's rights.

Fast forward to the 20th century, which witnessed several landmark victories for women's rights. The right to vote, gainful employment, and reproductive freedoms were hard-won achievements. But these gains did not come easily. They were met with fierce resistance. Patriarchal institutions, both secular and religious, fought tooth and nail to maintain their grip on power. Policies and laws were enacted to limit these newfound freedoms subtly. For example, women who joined the workforce during wartime were encouraged to return to 'domestic bliss' right after, sending a clear message: your place is in the home.

Even in contemporary times, the remnants of these oppressive paradigms persist. The gender pay gap, glass ceilings, and pervasive cultural stereotypes serve as modern shackles, tying women to antiquated roles. In many parts of the world, women still struggle for basic human rights, including education, freedom from violence, and reproductive autonomy. Global movements like #MeToo have brought these issues to the forefront, yet the battle is far from over. Each victory exposes new fronts in the ongoing war for fair and equal treatment.

Understanding the global historical paradigm of oppression is not just about recounting the past; it is about recognizing the deep-seated structures that continue to influence our present. It helps us see where we've been, so we know precisely where we need to go. By unearthing these buried truths, we gain the insight needed to foster genuine change—rooted in justice and equality.

As we reflect on this long history, it becomes clear that the winds of change are here. We're standing at a crucial juncture where oppression is no longer an unchallenged norm. The collective consciousness is awakening, driven by the voices of those who have endured generations of silence. This awakening is not just about reclaiming rights; it's about reclaiming the narratives that have long been written for us. It's about stepping into our power, rewriting the story, and ensuring that it is one of autonomy, strength, and unyielding resilience.

The global historical paradigm of oppression offers lessons in both suffering and triumph. It's a call to action—a urging us to break free from these chains, to challenge every form of subjugation, and to stand up for a future where women can thrive in the fullness of their potential. Now, more than ever, the winds of change are blowing, urging us to take bold steps toward everlasting freedom and empowerment.

CHAPTER 2:
THE GOAL OF THE PATRIARCHAL PARADIGM

In analyzing the patriarchal paradigm, it's essential to recognize that the primary goal is to sustain a balance of power skewed overwhelmingly in favor of men. This blueprint for dominance is not merely about visible oppression; it's about embedding a deep-seated belief that men are inherently entitled to authority, privilege, and control. By design, the patriarchal agenda aims to minimize women's presence in spaces of influence, whether in the boardroom, the political sphere, or within the confines of the home.

The patriarchal system thrives on sustaining hierarchies. These hierarchies are less about outright exclusion and more about creating an everlasting narrative of female inadequacy. The underlying shadow strategy involves manipulating societal norms and laws to reinforce power dynamics that favor men. By keeping women battling for basic rights and equality, the system distracts them from challenging the overarching patriarchal structure itself.

Intergenerational impacts of the patriarchy cannot be overstressed. From a mother's stifled ambitions to the learned helplessness of her daughter, and right down to the son who learns entitlement, the cycle perpetuates itself. Today's women—whether they realize it or not—are often the bearers of the wounds made by generations past. These wounds manifest as self-doubt, internalized misogyny, and even the silent acceptance of inequity.

Understanding the goal of the patriarchal paradigm brings us one step closer to dismantling it. We must remain vigilant about the subtle ways it infiltrates our lives, sewing seeds of division among women and seeking to keep us from uniting in our collective power. Generation by generation, the paradigm shapes societal norms, like whispers engrained in our minds, telling us what we should and shouldn't aspire to be.

Our task is not just to recognize the impact but to refuse to pass it on to future generations. The patriarchal paradigm weakens when women from all walks of life stand together, breaking through these imposed limitations and reclaiming their right to be heard. It is through unity, understanding, and mutual support that we can challenge and ultimately reverse these entrenched forces.

The Shadow Strategy of Power and Control/ Power & Privilege/ Entitlement

The Goal of the Patriarchal Paradigm, at its core, seeks to maintain and perpetuate power and control over women and marginalized communities. One of its most insidious tools is the Shadow Strategy of Power and Control, which thrives on subtleness and often goes unnoticed until its effects are deeply ingrained. This strategy works by embedding societal norms and values that uphold male dominance and privilege, thus creating an environment where entitlement and authority are seen as natural male traits. This conditioning not only suppresses the voices of women but also instills a sense of unearned privilege in men.

Through mechanisms of power and privilege, patriarchal systems perpetuate a cycle where women are continuously marginalized and their contributions undervalued. These systems rely heavily on social, economic, and political structures that prioritize male experiences and perspectives. Women are often pitted against one another, encouraged to compete for the limited spaces allowed to them. This fosters an environment where collective female empowerment is stifled, and individual achievements are burdened with the weight of exceptionalism, rather than being seen as part of a broader, united front for equality.

Entitlement, another arm of this shadow strategy, manifests in numerous ways, both overt and subtle. Men raised in patriarchal societies are often socialized to believe in their superiority and to expect rewards and deference as their right. This entitlement is evident in everyday scenarios, from dominating conversations to occupying leadership roles with an assumption of inherent competence. For women, breaking through such deeply entrenched entitlement requires not just individual resilience, but also a collective awakening and solidarity.

The Shadow Strategy also employs tactics of fear and manipulation to maintain control. By perpetuating myths about male superiority and female inadequacy, patriarchal systems create a culture of dependency and compliance. Women are often discouraged from aspiring towards leadership or independence, under the guise that their primary value lies in their relationships to men, be it as mothers, daughters, or wives. This is a deliberate attempt to keep women's potential and contributions minimalized and fragmented.

Yet, the resilience and wisdom of women have continuously challenged these shadowy tactics. By recognizing and naming these strategies, we are better equipped to dismantle them. Understanding how power, privilege, and entitlement function within a patriarchal framework empowers women to reject these limiting beliefs and to support one another in the quest for genuine equality. It is imperative that we internalize the knowledge that our worth is intrinsic and not defined by patriarchal standards.

The process of reclaiming autonomy over our bodies, minds, hearts, and spirits is both a personal and collective journey. This reclamation involves unlearning the internalized messages that suggest we are less-than and embracing the truth of our strengths and capabilities.

When we do this, we not only liberate ourselves-but also pave the way for future generations to experience a world where power is shared equitably, privilege is recognized and corrected, and entitlement is replaced with mutual respect and cooperation.

In essence, to counteract the patriarchal paradigm, we must continuously educate and empower ourselves and others. Change begins with awareness but is sustained through action. We can dismantle the shadow strategies of power and control by creating and nurturing spaces where all genders, especially women, can thrive without the limitations imposed by outdated and unfair systems. The path forward requires courage, unity, and an unwavering commitment to justice and equality.

Generational & Present-Day Impact to Women, Children & the Marginalized

Understanding the deeply ingrained patriarchal paradigm reveals how it perpetuates systematic oppression that affects women, children, and marginalized communities in both profound and sometimes subtle ways. Historically rooted in a desire for control and dominance, this power structure has cast a long shadow over countless generations, leaving scars that persist in present times. The repercussions have not dissipated with time; rather, they have shifted forms, adapting to modern contexts and challenges.

In earlier generations, patriarchal norms dictated every aspect of life for women and marginalized groups, from personal freedom to professional opportunities. Women were often confined to the domestic sphere, their worth measured in terms of their ability to bear and raise children, serve their husbands, and maintain households. Today, there is a distinct effort to return women to this era, beginning with controlling women's bodily autonomy. Marginalized communities faced, and still face, barriers to education, healthcare, and economic opportunities. Children growing up in these environments internalized these constraints, perpetuating the cycle of oppression.

Consider the narrative of a young girl in the 19th century who was denied education because it was deemed unnecessary for her gender. Translate that to today's world, and while girls have more access to education, they often encounter gender biases in curriculum, sports, and career counseling that subtly reinforce traditional roles. In many places, young girls are still discouraged from pursuing Science, Technology, Engineering, Mathematics fields, thus perpetuating gender stereotypes and limiting potential economic independence.

Children in marginalized communities grow up witnessing and experiencing systemic racism, economic disparities, and social exclusion. These young minds are shaped by the injustices their families face, impacting their mental and emotional well-being. The generational impact here is two-fold: it instills a sense of inferiority and limits access to opportunities that could otherwise break the cycle of poverty and marginalization. The residual effects are felt in their adulthood, where breaking free from these ingrained limitations requires immense effort and often faces societal and institutional resistance.

Present-day impacts manifest in various forms of gender inequity and discrimination. The wage gap, for instance, is a glaring example of how the patriarchal paradigm values male labor over female labor. Women, even in developed nations, earn considerably less than their male counterparts for the same roles, reflecting an enduring legacy of undervalued female work. This economic disparity extends to marginalized women, amplifying their struggle for financial independence and sovereignty.

The intersectionality of race, sexuality, and gender identity provides a more complex picture of how the patriarchal framework affects marginalized groups. Women of color, LGBTQ+ individuals, and those from economically disadvantaged backgrounds experience compounded discrimination. These intersecting oppressions create unique challenges that can't be addressed by generalized solutions focused only on gender. For instance, a black, queer woman might face not only gender discrimination but also racial and homophobic prejudices that intertwine to restrict her social and economic mobility.

Contrastingly, the fight against this paradigm is just as impactful. Women and marginalized groups are reclaiming their narratives and autonomy through activism, education, and community building. The rise of feminist movements, LGBTQ+ rights organizations, and advocacy for racial equality showcases the resistance against systemic oppression. The #MeToo movement, for example, has opened up global conversations about sexual harassment and abuse, holding perpetrators accountable and fostering a culture where victims are believed and supported.

Moreover, women and marginalized groups are making significant strides in leadership roles across various sectors. From politics to business, having more women, people of color, and members of the LGBTQ+ community in leadership positions not only disrupts the traditional power dynamics but also brings diverse perspectives that drive inclusive policies and practices. Such representation is crucial for creating an equitable society where everyone's voices are heard and valued.

The impact on future generations hinges on our collective will to dismantle these entrenched norms. Another less visible and spoken impact is the way internalized oppression causes the division and subsequent oppression of "others" within the same marginalized community. Education plays a critical role in this transformation, emphasizing equitable and inclusive curricula that celebrate diversity and teach respect and empathy from a young age. Empowering women, children, and marginalized groups through knowledge and resources can pave the way for a more just and nurturing world.

Understanding the generational and present-day impacts of the patriarchal paradigm is essential for devising strategies to combat its ongoing and lingering effects. It's a call to action for all of us to foster environments where every individual, regardless of gender, race, or background, can thrive. By addressing these deep-rooted issues, we move closer to a world where equity and empowerment aren't just ideals but lived realities.

CHAPTER 3:
OLD WAYS OF RESISTANCE TO OPPRESSION

Throughout history, women have found countless ways to resist oppression. These acts of defiance, both quiet and loud, are the backbone of our enduring fight for autonomy. Long before hashtags and social media campaigns, women used the tools available to them to make their voices heard and secure their rights, even when the odds were stacked against them.

In the shadows of societies dominated by patriarchal norms, women would gather in secret, sharing knowledge and providing support. These clandestine meetings were more than mere social gatherings; they were acts of rebellion. By coming together, 'women built' networks that fostered solidarity and created a sense of community, which was, in itself, a form of resistance.

Throughout different cultures, storytelling has been a powerful tool for challenging the status quo. Women passed down stories of resilience and courage, teaching future generations the importance of standing up against injustice. These narratives served as a reminder that the struggle for freedom and equality is not a new battle, but one that our foremothers have been fighting for centuries.

It is essential to recognize that old ways of resistance laid the groundwork for the triumphs we celebrate today. Historical victories, no matter how small, have taught us invaluable lessons. The backlash from patriarchal structures has often been severe, but each act of defiance has brought us closer to realizing our true power. Confronting oppression demanded bravery, and it taught us the importance of resilience and perseverance.

The wisdom gleaned from these past attempts is a treasure trove for our contemporary movements. Reflecting on the courage of those who came before us strengthens our resolve. We've learned that our true power lies within, in our ability to unite, support each other, and persist despite the challenges. The strength drawn from these old ways of resistance continues to inspire and empower us to fight for a future where all women can live freely and fully.

Victories and Patriarchal Reactions

Throughout history, women have celebrated numerous victories in their ongoing struggle against patriarchal oppression. These triumphs, big and small, have served as milestones in the journey toward greater autonomy and equality. Women's right to vote, the right to work, and the ability to hold property—all these achievements have been the results of brave, persistent efforts. Every victory, however, did not come without its own set of challenges and patriarchal reactions.

When women first began to organize and demand rights, the patriarchy responded with a mixture of fear and aggression. Suffragettes faced brutal force-feeding in prisons. Women attempting to enter male-dominated fields were greeted with blatant hostility and discrimination. These reactions were designed to instill fear and maintain control, reflecting a system that felt threatened by the idea of female empowerment. Indeed, every inch of progress challenged the status quo and forced society to confront deeply ingrained prejudices.

The backlash has often been swift and severe. When women secured the right to vote, there were immediate legislative attempts to undermine it through discriminatory policies and practices. The same pattern emerged when women entered the workforce in greater numbers during World War II, only to be pushed back into domestic roles as soon as the war ended. Each victory prompted a counteraction aimed at reasserting patriarchal dominance.

However, it is crucial to understand that these reactions are not just about maintaining power but also about fear. The fear that comes from losing a long-held control over society's structure. The fear of an awakened and empowered female force that refuses to be silenced. This fear has often manifested in attempts to discredit women's achievements, belittle their efforts, and perpetuate negative stereotypes.

Yet, despite these reactions, women have continued to advance. Each setback became a lesson, each reaction a catalyst for further action. The strength and resilience demonstrated by every woman who dared to defy the status quo have paved the way for future generations. These victories have created a ripple effect, inspiring change agents across different spheres of life to push for a more equitable and just world.

The triumphs of the past also underscore the importance of collective action. When women unify and stand together, their combined strength can challenge even the most entrenched systems of oppression. The goal is not just to secure rights but to foster a culture where true equality and respect can flourish. Patriarchal reactions, strenuous as they may be, reveal the cracks in the system and offer opportunities for further resistance and change.

Ultimately, the victories and the ensuing patriarchal reactions highlight a timeless truth: the struggle for gender equality is ongoing. Every gain must be vigilantly protected, every reaction must be met with renewed determination. We are facing another such moment and opportunity for true liberation now.

By learning from the past and understanding the dynamics of resistance and reaction, women can build resilient strategies to counter oppression. The journey may be fraught with obstacles, but each victory, no matter how small, marks a step closer to reclaiming autonomy over our bodies, minds, hearts, and spirits. Will we choose a path to sovereignty?

Consequences of Female Triumphs

Challenging the status quo and sparking significant change, the consequences of female triumphs have long reverberated through societies. When women achieve major victories, the ripples extend far beyond the immediate benefits, shaking the very foundations of patriarchal structures. This is not a tale of isolated incidents but a narrative of collective awakening, where every triumph pushes the needle closer to equitable sovereignty.

Historical accounts and contemporary events underscore that when women rise, they often stir a hornet's nest of opposition. Resistance can be fierce, manifesting in societal pushback, legal hurdles, and even personal backlash. For instance, when women first fought for the right to vote, they encountered virulent opposition, revealing deep-seated fears about losing control. These reactions, though harsh, are paradoxically a signal of progress—a forced confrontation with outdated paradigms.

Patriarchal backlash frequently seeks to penalize women for their success. It's more than just overt attempts to repeal rights; it subtly weaves through the fabric of daily life, manifesting as microaggressions or institutional biases. Think about how successful women are often socially branded: too assertive, too emotional, or too ambitious. While these labels aim to undercut their achievements, they're also evidence of a system grappling with change. Yet, every time a woman shatters a glass ceiling, she paves a smoother path for those who follow.

Triumphant women often confront what could be termed the "double burden." They're expected to excel not just professionally but also maintain traditional roles in their personal lives. This dual expectation reveals the systemic reluctance to adjust to new norms and roles. However, women have continually demonstrated that it's possible to balance these demands, thereby challenging and gradually redefining societal expectations.

Consider the impact of female triumphs on younger generations. When girls see women leading, whether it's in corporate boardrooms, scientific communities, or grassroots movements, they see what's possible. These role models don't just inspire; they create a blueprint for liberation. They teach that the fight for equality is worth every struggle and setback, and that each victory is a collective win. Such visibility has a profound effect, instilling confidence and ambition in the female leaders of tomorrow.

The triumphs of women also bring about a richer tapestry of perspectives in decision-making processes. Whether in politics, business, or community leadership, the inclusion of diverse voices ensures more holistic and just policies and practices. This inclusiveness challenges the monolithic nature of patriarchal governance and introduces a multiplicity of insights that ultimately benefit everyone within the society.

Economic empowerment is another significant consequence of female victories. Women achieving financial independence disrupt the traditional power dynamics within households and communities. Financial freedom can lead to greater self-determination, better opportunities for children, and a ripple effect that elevates families and communities. This shift not only enhances individual lives but also enriches the broader socio-economic fabric of society.

In the end, the consequences of female triumphs are as vast as they are transformative. They challenge the old, birthing new paradigms where equity and justice are within reach. Celebrate these victories, large and small, as milestones in a relentless journey toward a world where every woman's potential is not just recognized, but also revered and nurtured.

Wisdom Gained from Past Attempts

Throughout history, women have continuously fought against the shackles of oppression, drawing wisdom from each struggle to fuel the next. One of the most profound pieces of wisdom gleaned from these attempts is the power of resilience. Women have demonstrated time and again that, despite the adversities they face, they possess a strength that often surprises even themselves. This resilience isn't just about surviving; it's about thriving against the odds, showing that persistence in the face of oppression can gradually bend the arc of history toward justice.

An important lesson from past resistance is the value of solidarity. When women unite, their collective strength becomes an unassailable force. Individual battles, no matter how brave, often falter without communal support. The suffrage movement, civil rights activism, and contemporary feminist waves have all shown that systemic change requires a united front. Learning to see our struggles as interwoven rather than isolated helps to build a stronger, more cohesive movement.

Another vital insight is the importance of adaptability. Oppressive systems often morph and evolve, presenting different challenges over time. Successful resistance understands the necessity of evolving strategies. Historical movements have taught us to remain flexible, to reassess and redirect our efforts as needed. This adaptability has allowed us to outwit the oftentimes formidable forces of patriarchy, demonstrating that rigidity is the enemy of progress.

Additionally, past attempts at resistance have underscored the power of education and awareness. Knowledge equips us with the tools to dismantle false narratives and debunk myths perpetuated by patriarchal systems. The more we know about history, politics, and our own rights, the more effective our resistance becomes. Movements that have prioritized education, such as the Women's Liberation Movement of the 1960s and 70s, have seen substantial and lasting impacts. Information truly is power, and with it, we become capable of challenging the status quo.

Intergenerational wisdom has also emerged as a significant factor. The experiences and stories handed down from mothers to daughters, elders to the younger generation, form a rich tapestry of knowledge and strategies. These stories nurture a deep understanding that we are not isolated in our struggles; we are part of a continuing lineage of warriors who have fought and will continue to fight for equity. Drawing on this legacy not only honors those who came before us but also empowers us to forge ahead with greater confidence and clarity.

Equally important is the understanding that personal liberation is deeply tied to collective liberation. Women have learned that true freedom isn't just individual but communal. Each personal victory against oppression contributes to a larger mosaic of collective progress. This collective mindset fosters empathy, mutual support, and shared victories, creating a fertile ground for sustainable change.

Finally, the wisdom of maintaining hope amid despair shines through history like a beacon. Past attempts at resistance teach us that hope is not a passive wish but an active stance. It fuels resilience, determination, and innovation. Holding onto hope, even in the darkest times, has allowed women to envision a world that doesn't yet exist, guiding them to make that vision a reality. This wisdom reinforces the belief that, no matter how entrenched oppression may appear, change is always possible.

In synthesizing the wisdom from past attempts, we find a treasure trove of strategies, mindsets, and lessons that fortify our current and future efforts. The journey is ongoing, and each step forward is a tribute to the battles fought and the wisdom gained. Through understanding and applying these lessons, we arm ourselves with the inner power necessary to dismantle oppressive systems and reclaim our autonomy.

Our True Power Lies Within

An essential part of understanding the depth of our strength is the embrace of our true power which lies within us. When we're faced with the systemic barriers set up by patriarchal structures, it's natural to feel overwhelmed, but believe me, the power to overcome these lies within each of us. Recognizing this inherent power is the first step towards making lasting change. It's about knowing that the essence of who we are is not dependent on external validation, and our inner strength is a force that can ripple out to transform our lives and communities.

Understanding our true power requires a deep reflection on our individual and collective strengths. Often, society conditions us to minimize our capabilities or value, but the reality is quite the opposite. We possess an extraordinary capacity for resilience and wisdom that has been passed down through generations of women who have fought, survived, and thrived despite numerous challenges. *Every battle they fought, every victory they celebrated, and even every setback they encountered has woven into the fabric of our being, providing us with an arsenal of tools and insights.*

To harness this power, we must look inward and connect with our authentic selves. That means shedding the layers of self-doubt, fear, and imposed limitations. It's about embracing the wholeness of our experiences—both joyous and painful. The journey inward can be intimidating, but it's crucial. As we dig deep, we discover not only our strengths but also the untapped potential that has been lying dormant, waiting to be awakened.

Our true power lies within our ability to recognize and honor every aspect of our being. This includes reclaiming our voices and the right to tell our own stories. Too often, our narratives are reshaped or silenced by a patriarchal lens, but when we reclaim our stories, we reframe our experience in ways that empower us and inspire those around us. We need to reach out to each other, share our triumphs and struggles, and build a tapestry of support and solidarity.

In the grand scheme of things, the real revolution starts within. It's setting the stage for us to emerge as empowered beings ready to redefine our realities. Let's embrace the undeniable truth that our true power lies within and use it as the foundation for creating a world where we thrive unapologetically and irrevocably in control of our destinies.

CHAPTER 4:
THE LIBERATION OF
YOUR WHOLE SELF

Imagine a life where every part of you thrives—your body, mind, heart, and spirit in unison. This isn't a fantastical dream but an achievable reality. By liberating each part of ourselves, we pave the way for genuine autonomy. Centuries of societal conditioning have compelled us to compartmentalize our existence, leaving fragments of our true selves behind. This chapter is your guide to reclaiming these lost aspects.

Your body is your vessel, and it carries your wisdom, traumas, and joys. It's essential to start with self-awareness and acceptance. How many of us have felt shackled by unrealistic beauty standards or bodily expectations? Begin to see your body as more than a container. Intend to come into relationship with her-your SheBody. Embrace her strength and potential, honor her signals, and nourish her with respect. When you trust and honor your body as Sacred, you root your liberation in a solid, tangible reality.

Turning to the realm of the mind, it's crucial to identify and dismantle the mental chains that have held you back. These chains often take the form of self-doubt, fear, and internalized societal norms. Challenge these thoughts and replace them with affirmations of empowerment. Education and continuous learning through self-discovery, can be transformative. Engage in dialogues, journalling daily, read extensively, and expose yourself to diverse perspectives. In doing so, you create a powerful mind that not only questions but also acts.

Our hearts hold immense power, often buried under layers of hurt and disappointment. Vulnerability is not a weakness but a source of strength. Form meaningful connections with others on a similar journey of the heart. Practice empathy and allow yourself to feel profoundly, the suffering of another. It's in these genuine moments of connection where true healing happens, and your heart's liberation becomes palpable. Remember, love is not just for others but, importantly, for yourself.

The spirit, often the overlooked dimension, requires us to reprioritize our life's walk. It is the essence that connects us to something greater than ourselves. Whether through meditative practices, rituals, or spiritual communities, find what resonates with you. Nurture your spirit through creativity, nature, or acts of kindness. A liberated spirit radiates a sense of purpose, guiding all other aspects of your being in harmony.

As we navigate through this chapter, the liberation of your whole self is a journey, not a destination. Each step you take towards owning your body, mind, heart, and spirit is a step away from oppression and a leap towards empowerment. This wholeness is your birthright. Claim it, live it, and let it inspire others.

Owning Your Body, Mind, Heart & Spirit

Liberating your whole self involves taking full ownership of every aspect of who you are—mind, body, heart, and spirit-strengths and weaknesses. This ownership is critical in breaking free from the chains of patriarchal oppression. It means aligning each part of yourself with your true identity and reclaiming the power that has often been denied or suppressed.

The first step to owning your body is recognizing its sanctity and beauty. Many of us have been taught to disconnect from our physical selves due to societal standards, objectification, or trauma. It's essential to reconnect with your body, honor it, and listen to what it needs. This means paying attention to your senses, understanding your boundaries, and appreciating your physical form for all it does for you. Celebrate your body as the vessel that carries your essence and holds your strength.

Your mind is a powerful tool that shapes your reality. Owning your mind involves being aware of the thoughts, beliefs, and narratives that govern your life. It's about questioning inherited belief systems and discarding those that don't serve your higher purpose. Challenge these thoughts by asking yourself, "where did that thought come from? Is it mine or am I repeating something I heard?" Then, replace them with affirmations of empowerment that reflect YOUR thought or beliefs. Empowering your mind involves nurturing it with knowledge, stimulating it with creative ideas, and challenging it with critical thinking. It's also recognizing that mental health is as crucial as physical health; seek help and practice self-care to maintain mental well-being.

Owning your heart means embracing your emotions and understanding that vulnerability is not a weakness but a profound strength. In a world that often tells us to hide our feelings, reclaiming your emotional world means allowing yourself to feel deeply and authentically. Using creativity, a woman's medicine-to express, give perspective, release, heal, forgive, enlighten is a beautiful way to bring healing to the heart. Owning the language of your heart means acknowledging the pain and joy, the sorrow and happiness—all the facets that make your emotional experience rich and meaningful. Allow your heart to guide you in forming genuine connections and showing compassion to yourself and others.

Your spirit is the core of who you are, an eternal essence that transcends the physical world. It is a Divine connection with the Sacred Self within. It is a relationship with a Greater Love that nurtures, supports, holds our fears and hurts with a lovingkindness that keeps our hope alive. It is the kind of Love that makes you Brave enough to Own yourSelf. It contains the Love of Mother Earth, the Pachamama, the Divine Feminine Face of God, the Mother God. Owning your spirit involves recognizing your inherent worth and the unique gifts you bring to the world. It means tapping into your intuition, listening to your inner voice, and aligning your life choices with your soul's purpose. Spiritual ownership is about finding practices—be it meditation, prayer, nature walks, or creative expression—that connect you to something greater than yourself, nurturing your inner light.

To truly reclaim your autonomy, understand that these aspects of yourself—body, mind, heart, and spirit—are interconnected. When you nurture your body, your mind functions better. When you free your mind from limiting beliefs, your heart can open up to new possibilities. When your heart is full, your spirit shines brightly. Every self-care act furthers the journey towards liberation.

Achieving autonomy over these areas requires ongoing reflection and active commitments. This is the essential first part of the journey. It's not a one-time event but a continuous practice throughout this transformational journey. Challenge the status quo, rise against internalized oppression, and embody the full spectrum of who you are. Doing so not only liberates you personally but also sets a powerful example for others to follow. Your journey to wholeness can inspire a collective shift, creating ripples of change that reach far beyond your immediate sphere.

In celebrating and integrating your whole self, you're laying the groundwork for a new world where every woman can stand in her power and thrive. Your journey serves as a beacon of hope and a call to action, urging others to do the same. This collective liberation bridges our individual paths into a unified quest for true freedom.

Where Are You NOT Free? What Part of You Do You NOT Own?

These medicine questions are critical inquiries of the self, that demand deep personal reflection. In many ways, society has conditioned us to submit to roles and expectations that stifle our authenticity. Think about the various aspects of your life: your thoughts, your decisions, and even your dreams. How many of these are genuinely yours, and how many have been influenced by societal norms? When we start dissecting these layers, we often discover that our freedom has been compromised in more ways than we initially perceived.

Reflect on your body. Have you ever felt compelled to alter your appearance to fit a predefined mold of beauty? The relentless pursuit of an 'ideal' body often distorts our self-image, making us believe we're never good enough. Advertisements, social media, and even well-meaning advice from loved ones can impose views that lock us in a perpetual state of self-criticism. Your body is your temple, and yet, how often do you feel a genuine sense of ownership over it?

Consider your mind. Are your beliefs and values truly your own, or have they been shaped by the echo chamber of cultural and familial expectations? From a young age, we're inundated with messages about what a woman should be, think, and aspire to achieve. These external influences can constrict the mental freedom we need to explore our true selves. Breaking free from these mental chains requires an ongoing commitment to self-discovery and the courage to question long-held assumptions.

Your heart and spirit are also arenas where freedom can be elusive. Relationships, whether romantic, familial, or platonic, often come with expectations that might not align with our true selves. Have you ever stayed in a relationship because you felt it was your duty, rather than a choice born from genuine love and connection? Spirituality too, can be hijacked by dogma and institutionalized beliefs. True liberation means reclaiming your heart's desires and spiritual truths, even if they diverge from what you've been taught.

Ultimately, identifying where you're not free and the parts of you that you do not own is the first step toward reclaiming your autonomy. It's a journey of peeling back the layers of societal conditioning to reveal the essence of who you are. Embracing this journey is not just a personal act of revolution; it's a radical step that contributes to dismantling the larger framework of oppression that holds so many women back. We must stop waiting for the patriarchy to give us permission to own that which was ours to begin with. By owning every part of yourself—your body, mind, heart, and spirit—you set a powerful example for others to follow, catalyzing a collective movement toward genuine liberation and equality.

Choosing Who You Are

In reclaiming our autonomy, it begins with a profound act of self-definition. It's about choosing who you are, not based on societal expectations or inherited roles, but on an authentic understanding of your own essence. This journey requires introspection and courage, but it offers unparalleled liberation. The first step is recognizing that you possess the power to define yourself beyond external labels and imposed identities.

Is your identity shaped by others' perceptions? If so, it's time to reframe your narrative. Think about the aspects of yourself you truly value and recognize that those are what make you unique and powerful. Take a moment to consider: What are the qualities, passions, and values that resonate most with your core? By grounding yourself in these, you reclaim your narrative and fortify your sense of self.

Remember, you don't have to fit into predefined molds. Embrace the fluidity of identity; it's okay to evolve. The essence of who you are can shift as you grow, learn, and experience new things. There's immense power in embracing your dynamic identity, in allowing yourself to be influenced by positive changes while maintaining your inner truth. Our true selves are multifaceted and ever-changing, akin to a prism reflecting different hues depending on the light.

Choosing who you are also compels you to confront the parts of yourself that you may have neglected or suppressed due to societal pressures. Maybe there's a creative force within you yearning for expression, or a spirit of leadership waiting to emerge. By acknowledging and nurturing these aspects, you unlock a fuller version of yourself. This isn't merely an intellectual exercise but a heartfelt commitment to living authentically.

Finally, your identity should be a source of empowerment, not confinement. By consciously choosing who you are, you break free from the shackles of patriarchal expectations and step into a space where your body, mind, heart, and spirit are sovereign. This liberation sets the stage for you to live a life rich with purpose, passion, and truth, inspiring those around you to embark on their own journeys of self-discovery and empowerment.

You are NOT Your Trauma

Your trauma is not who you are. It does not define you. It is what happened to you. It may impact aspects of your daily life experience, but it doesn't determine your worth or your identity. As women navigating a world often starkly affected by patriarchal conditioning, abuses of power and violations of the personal self, it's essential to distinguish between what has happened to us and who we truly are. Drawing this line empowers us to reclaim parts of ourselves that have been overshadowed by past wounds. Trauma might be a chapter in your life, but it is not the title of your story.

Internalized trauma can obscure the beauty of the present and blind us to future possibilities. However, by recognizing that you are not the sum of your traumatic experiences, you begin to dismantle the hold it has over you. Empowerment begins with self-recognition. Realizing that the essence of your being remains intact despite any past harm opens doors to emotional freedom and self-actualization. It is an act of reclamation, an assertion that your true self still possesses all its innate power.

Examine the ways in which your trauma may have altered your perceptions and responses. Understand that these adaptations were survival mechanisms, but they don't need to become permanent fixtures in your life. The path to greater autonomy starts when you allow yourself to be seen as a whole person, beyond the confines of painful memories. Acknowledge your trauma without it becoming a label that limits your potential.

Take conscious steps toward releasing the grip of trauma by fostering resilience and self-compassion. Embrace the parts of yourself that have emerged strong and steadfast despite, or perhaps because of, your experiences. Nourish these aspects and allow them to grow, creating a new narrative that celebrates your ongoing journey toward wholeness. Each step forward is a declaration of your sovereignty over your mind, heart, body, and spirit.

By redefining your relationship with trauma, you transform it from a source of pain into a reservoir of strength. Recognize that your story is still unfolding, filled with chapters of love, joy, and immense capacity for change. Embrace your power, not because of what happened to you, but because of who you inherently are. You are not your trauma; you are the force of life that persists, thrives, and continues to blossom.

CHAPTER 5:
TRANSFORMING TRAUMA INTO POWER

It's time to recognize the immense resiliency that's birthed from surviving trauma. Acknowledging pain isn't easy, but it's crucial. By facing the hurt head-on, we start to identify the strengths we've built along the way. These strengths are the bedrock of our power, a testament to our unyielding spirit. Think of every tear shed, every moment of self-doubt, as a transformative milestone, turning raw wounds into battle scars of empowerment.

Trauma can often feel like it holds us back, shackling us to the past. But when we confront it, we find the seeds of change hidden within. Our survival is not a sign of mere endurance; it's proof of our extraordinary capacity for resilience. These experiences cultivate in us empathy, courage, and a depth of understanding that can drive progressive change.

Our pain and the strength born from it can serve as catalysts for change. When we utilize these strengths, we find purpose and direction. This isn't a passive journey; it's an active transformation. We use our stories to fuel our endeavors, crafting a narrative where we shift from victims to victors.

Communities of women have long been the bastions of collective strength. As we share our stories, we create a tapestry of experiences that both honor our past and look toward our future. We become empowered storytellers, using our pain as a platform to inspire and instigate change not just for ourselves, but for others too.

Personal trauma, when addressed, becomes a of insights and medicine bag full of skills. These aren't just personal assets but societal gifts. Our power lies in sharing these gifts, in turning individual struggles into collective action and support. Embrace this power. Let your personal transformation be the spark that lights the way for others to follow.

Acknowledging Pain and Strengths Gained in the Survival

Acknowledging pain is often the first steppingstone toward true healing and transformation. Recognizing the wounds inflicted by patriarchal structures is crucial, not just to understand our struggles but to harness the strength that emerges from enduring them. In a world dominated by systemic oppression, women have often had to navigate a labyrinth of challenges. The scars from these experiences can sometimes feel like a burden, but within those scars lies a story of survival, resilience, and immense power.

For many, the pain manifests in different shapes and forms—be it physical, emotional, or psychological. The process of acknowledging this pain isn't about dwelling in victimhood; it's about recognizing the battles fought and the strength it took to endure them. It's about giving space to our lived experiences and understanding that through every struggle, we were unknowingly forging our inner warriors.

Survival, in essence, is a testament to our enduring spirit. The very act of rising each day despite life's adversities is a display of courage. However, surviving isn't just about getting through; it also involves embracing the lessons learned along the way. Every experience, no matter how painful, brings with it a gift of insight and strength. When we dare to acknowledge our pain, we begin to see the depths of our resilience and the surprising strengths we developed.

Consider the journey of a woman who has navigated the terrain of emotional abuse. Initially, her pain may seem overwhelming, but as she begins to understand and process it, she discovers the strength she developed in standing up for herself. She realizes that her empathy for others in similar situations has deepened, and she finds a newfound ability to advocate for those who may be struggling. In this way, her trauma isn't just a source of pain; it becomes a source of power and purpose.

Furthermore, shared experiences of pain and survival can become a bonding force within sisterhoods. When women come together to share their stories, they create a collective tapestry of resilience. This shared understanding paves the way for mutual support and collective healing. It allows women to see that they're not alone in their struggles and that they can draw strength from each other's journeys.

In this transformative process, the importance of acknowledging not just the pain but also the strengths gained in survival cannot be overstated. Every woman has a unique story, a unique struggle, and consequently, unique strengths. Whether it's the ability to navigate complex emotional landscapes, the resilience to rebuild after a loss, or the courage to confront injustice—each of these strengths is a testament to a woman's power.

This isn't about minimizing the pain or romanticizing the struggle. Rather, it's about shifting perspective to see the pain as a catalyst for growth and recognizing the strengths developed in the process. It's about empowering women to look at their experiences and say, "This shaped me into who I am today, and I am stronger because of it." In acknowledging both pain and strength, we reclaim our narratives and transform trauma into a wellspring of power.

Catalysts for Change: Using Strengths to Fuel Purpose

In the journey of transforming trauma into power, it is crucial to recognize the inherent strengths that have allowed survival and resilience. Trauma, despite its harrowing effects, often forges traits like perseverance, empathy, and unwavering courage. These strengths are the raw materials for personal and collective transformation. Acknowledging these qualities isn't just a step in healing; it's a revolutionary act of reclaiming one's narrative and purpose.

Harnessing these strengths begins with an intimate understanding of one's capabilities and how they can be channeled towards a greater purpose. Here, the intersection of self-awareness and action becomes a catalyst for change. It starts with small, conscious decisions—choosing to speak up in places where silence was once a refuge, setting boundaries where there were none, and daring to dream in spaces where hope seemed dim. These acts might appear minor individually, but collectively, they set the pace for profound transformation.

Consider the countless women who have used their experiences of hardship as a launching pad for social action. They often discover that the pain endured has fine-tuned their sense of justice and empathy, compelling them to advocate not just for themselves, but for others too. Their stories remind us that our personal journeys are deeply intertwined with broader social movements. Individual strength thus becomes the sinew binding community action—each effort reinforcing the other.

Strengths gained from overcoming trauma also empower effective leadership. When women step into roles of influence, their unique insights into human vulnerability and resilience can guide compassionate, inclusive governance. This leadership isn't about wielding power over others; it's about inspiring and uplifting those around them. It's about creating spaces where others can see their own potential for transformation, igniting a ripple effect of empowerment.

Moreover, understanding one's strengths creates a robust foundation for building networks of support and solidarity. When women come together, aware of their collective power and individual talents, they form formidable alliances that can challenge even the most entrenched systems of oppression. These networks are lifelines, offering not just support but also a sense of shared purpose and direction. In this sisterhood, every woman's strength complements another's, forging an unbreakable chain of empowerment.

Yet, using strengths to fuel purpose also involves facing the shadows within. It takes courage to confront internalized beliefs that may hinder one's growth. These beliefs, often seeded by patriarchal conditioning, can diminish self-worth and sabotage potential. Acknowledging and dismantling these barriers is essential for unlocking the full spectrum of one's capabilities. This process is neither swift nor easy, but it is profoundly liberating and necessary for sustained change.

Ultimately, the goal is not only personal empowerment but collective liberation. As each woman discovers and harnesses her strengths, she becomes a beacon of possibility for others. Her journey of transformation serves as a testament to the boundless potential within all of us to fuel our purpose. Through this shared endeavor, we create a world where women's strengths are celebrated, and their purposes collectively elevate society. The power to change, to heal, to lead, and to inspire resides in each of us—our strengths are the catalysts, and our purpose is the path.

CHAPTER 6:
HEALING SISTERHOOD WOUNDS

The bonds of sisterhood, once a source of unity and strength, have been strained under the weight of internalized patriarchy. We often find ourselves competing, judging, and distancing from one another in ways that perpetuate the very structures of oppression we're trying to dismantle. But recognizing these wounds is the first step toward healing.

Internalized patriarchy manifests subtly, embedding itself in our interactions and thoughts. When we catch ourselves doubting another woman's capabilities, questioning her choices, or feeling the urge to diminish her accomplishments, we're witnessing this internalized belief in action. It's crucial to realize that these thoughts aren't innate; they're learned. Where did the original belief about the inadequacy of women come from? This is the ongoing legacy of the patriarchy-to set women against each other-to battle one another...thus diminishing our collective power. It was and is learned-and what is learned can be unlearned.

Our societal conditioning has taught us to see each other as rivals instead of allies. This rivalry is rooted deeply in a scarcity mindset, the belief that there isn't enough success, love, or opportunity to go around. This belief supports the patriarchal hold on power. However, we must challenge and transcend this mindset by reminding ourselves that another woman's success does not diminish our own. The more we support and elevate each other, the stronger we become collectively.

Healing these wounds requires intention and effort. Start with personal reflection. Identify when and why you might have felt threatened by another woman. Was it her confidence, her beauty, her intelligence? Acknowledging these moments can be uncomfortable, but it's necessary for growth. Next, practice empathy and compassion. Put yourself in her shoes. Know that you do not know her story. Allow yourself to understand that every woman, like you, is on her own journey, facing her own struggles, and doing the best she can with the tools she has.

Engage in open and honest conversations with your sisters. Create spaces where vulnerability is met with support, rather than judgment. Remember that judgment defines the judger, NOT the judged. When we share our insecurities and fears, we not only unburden ourselves but also allow others to see that they are not alone. This builds deeper connections and fosters a sense of solidarity.

Strengthening our sisterhood is not just about healing individually, but also about empowering our collective ability to enact change. As we mend these hoops of trust and mutual respect, we fortify our impact in challenging and transforming the patriarchal structures around us. Together, we can create a world where every woman feels seen, heard, and valued. It is our unified, collective power that is the dissolution of the patriarchy's hold on power and control over our sovereignty. Our healing and unity is the path toward our collective sovereignty.

Recognizing Internalized Patriarchy

In the journey of healing sisterhood wounds, recognizing internalized patriarchy is crucial. Internalized patriarchy manifests as the oppressive norms and beliefs that women unconsciously adopt and perpetuate, often without realizing the damaging effects on themselves and others. It's about the subtle yet pervasive ways we might undermine ourselves and our sisters, reinforcing the very structures we aim to dismantle.

Consider the societal expectations ingrained in us from a young age: to compete against one another, to judge each other's choices, appearances, and abilities. These actions aren't merely personal failings but are reinforced by a historical context designed to keep women divided and conquered. By understanding and identifying these patterns, we can begin the work of deconstructing them within ourselves and our communities.

Yet, recognizing internalized patriarchy is not just about identifying harmful beliefs—it's about unlearning them. It requires deep introspection and a willingness to confront uncomfortable truths about our own behavior and mindset. Ask yourself: In what ways do I perpetuate stereotypes about other women? How often do I find myself doubting or diminishing my own worth based on patriarchal standards? Search social media for examples of these kind of comments/judgments made by women about women...examples of internalized patriarchal myths. Likewise, search for examples where liberated, sovereign women's comments lift up women. These questions can open the door to greater self-awareness and collective healing.

The work of unlearning patriarchal conditioning is intertwined with the broader movement for women's empowerment. When we free ourselves from these internal chains, we create the space for authentic connections and mutual upliftment. We become stronger, more compassionate allies to one another. This is the essence of healing sisterhood wounds—acknowledging the pain, understanding its origins, and intentionally choosing a new path forward.

Breaking away from internalized patriarchy empowers us to reclaim our full potential. It allows us to rewrite the narrative—one where women support, celebrate, and champion each other. This transformation doesn't happen overnight, but each step taken in mindfulness and solidarity moves us closer to a world where sisterhood thrives, unburdened by the shackles of oppression.

Understanding How We Cause Harm to Our Sisterhood

To understand the harm, we sometimes inflict on our own sisterhood, can seem like a deep and sometimes uncomfortable journey, but it's one we must undertake. Internalized patriarchy has, for centuries, driven wedges between us, fostering competition rather than collaboration, and criticism instead of compassion. To break free from these chains, we need to first recognize the subtle and not-so-subtle ways in which we might be perpetuating harm among ourselves.

First, let's talk about envy. It's whispered in hallways and screamed in silent glances. We often envy each other's successes, not realizing that each woman's victory is a win for all of us in the struggle against patriarchal confines. Tearing each other down because of perceived competition only weakens our collective power. Lift your sister up when she reaches a milestone. Her triumph is a beacon guiding all of us towards greater possibilities.

Another significant issue is judgment. We've been conditioned to judge each other harshly, scrutinizing appearance, choices, and lifestyles. But this judgment is a tool of the patriarchy, a way to keep women divided and distracted from larger battles. Instead of judging, practice empathy. Understand that every woman's journey is unique, shaped by her own struggles and triumphs. Imagine what could be achieved if, instead of passing judgment, we offered support and encouragement.

Language, too, holds power in how we either uplift or harm our sisterhood. Words can be weapons or they can be the balm that heals wounds. Be mindful of how you speak about other women, especially when they're not around to defend themselves. Gossip and derogatory remarks, forms of verbal abuse, only serve to fracture our unity. Transform your words into tools of empowerment, using them to build bridges rather than walls.

We must also confront internalized misogyny. It's sneaky and persistent, manifesting in ways that sometimes escape our notice. When we believe that certain 'male' traits are superior to 'female' ones, we diminish the power inherent in our womanhood. Celebrate both tenderness and strength, intellect and intuition. Embrace the full spectrum of qualities we possess as gender-female individuals.

Then there's the matter of intersectionality. The feminist movement must be inclusive. Recognizing the unique struggles faced by women of different races, sexual orientations, and socio-economic backgrounds is crucial. When we focus our activism only on issues affecting a privileged few, we inadvertently cause harm by neglecting others within our sisterhood. True sisterhood demands inclusivity and the willingness to fight for the rights of all women.

We can't overlook the influence of self-doubt either. Societal pressures can lead us to undermine our own worth and capabilities, and in turn, we may project this doubt onto others. Instead, let's work to foster a culture of confidence. Encourage your sisters to pursue their passions and believe in their power. Remember, self-love and mutual support aren't just personal choices; they're acts of rebellion against a system designed to keep us subdued.

Understanding how we cause harm to our sisterhood is the first solid step towards healing and unity. By addressing envy, judgment, language, internalized misogyny, intersectionality, and self-doubt, we can begin to mend the wounds that have kept us apart. Together, we become an unstoppable force, capable of dismantling the structures of patriarchy and building a world where every woman thrives. Initiating this transformation within ourselves paves the way for a collective awakening, one that strengthens our ability to change the world.

Healing These Hoops Strengthens Our Ability to Change the World

The power that lies within the bonds of sisterhood is undeniable. These relationships have the potential to drive enormous change, both personally and globally. However, the wounds we harbor from sisterhood can often inhibit our ability to harness this power. Healing these hoops is crucial not only for our personal well-being but also for our collective impact on the world.

Patriarchy has done more than just oppress women; it has implanted seeds of discord among us. The competition for approval, the silent judgments, and the internalized sense of inferiority have built invisible walls. These wounds turn potential allies into adversaries, weakening the force that could otherwise galvanize major social transformations. It's time to break down these barriers and reclaim the solidarity that is our natural state.

Recognizing and addressing the internalized patriarchy that perpetuates these wounds is the first step. We must ask ourselves, "How have I contributed to the pain of my sister?" This kind of self-inquiry isn't about self-blame, it's about self-awareness and responsibility. By identifying how we've been conditioned to view other women as threats or competitors, we start the healing process. Awareness leads to change, and change leads to strength.

Healing these hoops isn't just about personal growth; it's about collective liberation. When we can look at another woman, not as a rival but as a partner, a collaborator, the possibilities become endless. A united sisterhood can challenge oppressive systems, create new paradigms of leadership, and inspire transformative action. This doesn't mean we won't have disagreements; rather, our focus shifts from tearing each other down to lifting each other up.

It's essential to create safe spaces for honest conversations, where women can share their experiences without fear of judgment. Setting the groundwork for trust and empathy can create a ripple effect. Once one woman feels supported and seen, she becomes a beacon for others. This is how movements begin, not with isolated acts but through interconnected webs of support and empowerment.

Moreover, healing these relationships empowers us to reclaim our autonomy in every aspect of our lives. When we know that our sisters have our backs, we're more likely to take bold steps towards our goals. This collective strength emboldens us to own our bodies, minds, hearts, and spirits fully. We become unstoppable forces for good, capable of altering the course of history.

Imagine a world where women no longer feel the need to undermine one another but instead celebrate each other's victories and support each other's journeys. This vision isn't just a utopian dream; it's a tangible possibility. It begins with healing the wounds inflicted by patriarchy and cultivating a sisterhood rooted in love and mutual respect. From this fertile ground, we can nurture the seeds of global change.

Our shared pain, when transformed into collective healing, becomes our greatest strength. United, we can dismantle the very structures designed to keep us apart. As we heal these hoops, we fortify our ability to not only change our personal narratives but also to revolutionize our communities and the world at large. Let's lean into this process, embrace each other fully, and change the world together.

CHAPTER 7:
WAYSHOWERS AND TRUTHTELLERS

In the heart of every movement for change, there are those who illuminate our path and speak truths that resonate in our core. These WayShowers and Truthtellers embody the art of compassionate understanding, guiding us with grace and resilience. They remind us that true leadership stems from a place of vulnerability and empathy, urging us to lead from the heart. As we listen to their stories, we learn that embracing our own voices and speaking our truths is not just an act of courage but a necessity for collective liberation. The power to change the world lies within each of us, waiting to be unlocked through honest dialogue and a commitment to our shared humanity. Let us honor these guiding lights, allowing their wisdom to inspire us to step into our own power and create a world where every woman's voice is heard and valued.

Compassionate Understanding Guides the Way

Compassion isn't just a value; it's a transformative force. As WayShowers and Truthtellers, we recognize that compassionate understanding is fundamental to guiding us through the maze of societal expectations and injustices. When we open our hearts to one another, listening intently and acknowledging each other's struggles, we foster a sense of unity that can move mountains. This kind of deep empathy creates a supportive environment where every woman can thrive, feel validated, and be encouraged to reclaim her autonomy.

Imagine a world where we lead with compassion rather than judgment. It begins with us choosing to understand before seeking to be understood. Such understanding dissolves the barriers constructed by patriarchal norms, elegantly countering centuries of division. Together, we identify our shared experiences and the common threads that bind us together, making our collective journey more powerful and more profound.

Every one of us carries a story filled with challenges and triumphs. By practicing compassionate understanding, we provide a safe haven for these stories to be told and honored. Compassion allows us to see beyond external differences and recognize that any woman's pain is our pain, her joy our joy. This perspective is essential for creating a sisterhood that supports and uplifts, rather than divides and competes.

Moreover, compassionate understanding isn't about weakness; it's about strength. It's about having the insight to know that someone else's success does not diminish our own. It is the foundation upon which we build the resilience needed to challenge entrenched systems of oppression. When we lead with this kind of open-hearted empathy, we naturally emerge as beacons of hope and change.

Let us then be the WayShowers who illuminate the path with our compassion, showing the world that leadership infused with empathy is not only possible but vital. In being compassionate WayShowers and Truthtellers, we lay down the tracks for a more just, loving, and equitable society, one where every woman can realize her true potential.

Heart Centered Leadership; Learning From Their Journeys

Learning from those who have gone before us, has become a vital cornerstone in the reclamation of autonomy for women. To truly harness the lessons of heart-centered leadership, we need to look closely at the journeys of women who have already walked that path. These are individuals who have faced immense challenges yet managed to lead with compassion, empathy, and an unyielding commitment to change. They remind us that courage isn't the absence of fear but the triumph over it.

One profound lesson we glean from their stories is the power of vulnerability. Embracing our vulnerabilities allows us to connect deeply with others, fostering environments where trust and authentic relationships can thrive. In a world often dominated by competition and hierarchy, these women show us that leading from the heart can dismantle barriers and build bridges. Their journeys demonstrate that leadership rooted in genuine care and mutual respect is not only possible but incredibly effective.

These heart-centered leaders continually turn inward, asking themselves hard questions and seeking to understand their own experiences and traumas. This inner work is crucial because it translates into outer actions that are congruent with their values. It's an invitation for us to undertake the same journey of self-discovery and self-acceptance. When we understand our own pain and journey, we can better empathize with and lead others.

Among those leaders is a common thread of authenticity. They embrace their true selves and show up fully, flaws and all. This authenticity creates a magnetic force around them, attracting like-minded individuals and sparking movements grounded in genuine connections. Their stories encourage us to drop the masks we wear and to step fully into who we are, thereby empowering others to do the same.

Heart-centered leadership also implies a commitment to continuous learning and growth. These women don't claim to have all the answers. Instead, they approach life with curiosity and openness, always willing to learn from others and adapt. Their humility and willingness to grow serve as critical reminders that leadership is a journey, not a destination.

Furthermore, these leaders exemplify resilience. They teach us that setbacks and failures are just temporary stops on the path to success. Their ability to rise again, often stronger than before, is perhaps one of the most inspiring aspects of their journeys. This resilience is not just personal but collective; they lift others as they rise, creating a ripple effect that extends beyond their immediate circles.

In essence, the journey of heart-centered leaders is characterized by a shared vision of a more compassionate and just world. They are torchbearers, lighting the way for us to follow with steadfast resolve and tender hearts. They remind us that to lead others effectively, we must first lead ourselves with integrity, compassion, and unwavering dedication.

The stories of these heart-centered leaders serve as not just lessons but profound calls to action. They urge us to step into our power and to lead from a place of love and empathy. As we reflect on their journeys, we find the inspiration to write our own stories of transformation, healing, and leadership. They show us that change begins within but ultimately flourishes when shared with others. In this collective journey, we reclaim not only our autonomy but our interconnectedness and shared humanity.

Speaking from the Heart's Vulnerabilities

In the pursuit of genuine leadership and impactful truth-telling, we must recognize that true strength often arises from acknowledging our vulnerabilities. To speak from the heart is not merely to share emotion; it's an act of courage, a revelation of our deepest truths. It's about opening up the parts of ourselves that we might usually guard and finding empowerment in that expression.

Heart-centered leadership demands this kind of vulnerability. When we allow ourselves to be seen in our entirety, we offer authenticity and build trust. This trust becomes the foundation upon which we can foster real change. In sharing our stories and our pain, we connect with others on a profound level, creating a tapestry of shared experiences that strengthens us collectively.

Embracing vulnerability isn't about exposing weakness; it's about harnessing our strength from those very parts of ourselves we might fear are fragile. Our hearts hold immense wisdom, and it's in the honesty of saying, "this is where I hurt," or "this is what I fear," that we can invite others to do the same. When we own our vulnerabilities, we become a beacon for those around us, guiding them towards their own truths.

There's a unique power in owning your voice, speaking your truth from the heart. It's an act of defiance against a society that often values facade over sincerity. By consciously choosing to lead from this place of integrity, we dismantle the expectations placed upon us by the patriarchy. In doing so, we reclaim parts of ourselves that have been stifled or suppressed.

The heart, in all its vulnerability, is a source of unparalleled strength. It teaches us compassion, empathy, and resilience. Speaking from this place, we transform our pain into purpose, our fears into fortitude. Each time we share our truths, we break down barriers and create an inclusive space for communal healing and personal empowerment. Let your heart's vulnerabilities be your guide, illuminating the path towards a brighter, more liberated future for us all.

Owning Your Voice; Truth Lives in the Heart

Your voice matters. It is about reconnecting with the most genuine part of yourself. Your voice is more than the sounds you make; it's the expression of your innermost truths. In a world that often tries to tell you what to think, feel, and say, claiming ownership of your voice becomes an act of radical defiance. It's a declaration of your unique perspective and a testament to your lived experiences.

Understanding that truth lives in the heart requires deep introspection. You must sift through the noise of external expectations and societal norms to uncover what truly matters to you. This process often involves confronting uncomfortable truths about your feelings, desires, and beliefs. It means being vulnerable enough to acknowledge your fears and courageous enough to speak your truth despite them.

Consider how many times you've bitten your tongue to avoid conflict or stayed silent out of fear of judgment. Each time you suppress your voice, a piece of your authentic self...folds inwards. This act of self-silencing is a form of oppression that perpetuates the patriarchal paradigm. To break free, you must cultivate a practice of consistently aligning your speech with your heart's truth. This isn't just about speaking out but speaking authentically, from a place of integrity and sincerity.

There's immense power in vulnerability. When you speak from the heart, you invite others to do the same. By owning your voice, you create a ripple effect that encourages others to find and express their truths. This collective authenticity can dismantle the structures of power and control that thrive on silence and compliance.

Owning your voice also means standing up for your beliefs and values, even when they're unpopular. True empowerment lies in the ability to articulate your thoughts and feelings clearly and confidently. It's about reclaiming the narrative of your life, rewriting it in your words, and refusing to let anyone else dictate your story.

To practice owning your voice, start by creating spaces where you feel safe to express yourself. Surround yourself with supportive individuals who value and respect your truth. Engage in activities that promote self-reflection such as journaling, meditation, or engaging in meaningful conversations. These practices help you tap into your inner wisdom, fostering a deeper connection with your heart's truths.

Learning to discern which battles to fight and which to let go is also crucial. Not every moment requires you to raise your voice, but when the stakes are high, and your integrity is on the line, speaking out becomes a necessity. It's in these moments that your voice has the potential to inspire, heal, and transform not just your life, but the lives of others.

Remember, your voice is unique. It carries the weight of your experiences, dreams, and aspirations. By owning it, you honor your journey and contribute to a larger tapestry of collective wisdom. Truth lives in the heart, but it's through your voice that it comes to life, creating a powerful resonance that can change the world.

CHAPTER 8:
THE DREAM MAKERS AND
WISDOMKEEPERS

In every epoch, women have emerged as the dream makers and the guardians of wisdom, safeguarding both the aspirations of future generations and the learnings of those who came before. These roles, though often understated or ignored by historical narratives, lie at the core of our collective progress. Today's journey isn't merely about envisioning a brighter future; it's about preserving and honoring the legacy that empowers that vision.

Our foremothers faced insurmountable challenges, yet they held steadfast to their dreams. They are the roots from which we draw our strength. By listening to their whispers of resilience, we embrace an ancient yet ever-renewing wisdom, a testament to their undying spirit. It's this continuity that transforms yesterday's struggles into tomorrow's strengths.

As visionaries, dream makers see the world not only as it is but as it could be. This ability to combine critical insight with hopeful imagination is a powerful catalyst for change. Their dreams are not frivolous fantasies but blueprints created from the fragments of past experiences—both victories and failures. These blueprints offer us a pathway, guiding our steps toward a more just and compassionate society.

The WisdomKeepers, on the other hand, are the narrators of our stories, ensuring that the invaluable lessons of their journeys carry forward. They remind us that the answers we seek have often been discovered by those who walked before us. By embracing and passing down this wisdom, we arm the next generation with the knowledge they need to forge their path. They become the living bridges, connecting the past and future in an unbroken chain of enlightenment.

To genuinely reclaim our autonomy, we must embody both the dream maker and the WisdomKeeper within ourselves. It's a tandem dance of innovation and tradition, making sure that our aspirations are deeply rooted in the soils of accumulated wisdom. This allows us to create not just for ourselves, but for countless generations of women to come.

Just as every tree bears the imprint of its growth rings, so too do our movements and dreams carry the imprints of the women who came before us. Let us honor them by becoming the guardians of our shared legacy, ensuring that it continues to grow, flourish, and inspire.

Visionaries of Tomorrow's World

The future belongs to those who dare to dream and boldly chart new paths. Women, long sidelined by patriarchal structures, are uniquely positioned to become visionaries of tomorrow's world. These visionary women see beyond the confines of present circumstances, understanding that their power lies not in conforming but in boldly pushing boundaries. They're the dream makers, the ones who believe in the power of collective change and the wisdom that stems from shared experiences.

For too long, society has dictated what women can and cannot achieve, boxing them into predefined roles. But visionaries see through these limitations, recognizing that the essence of change starts within. They harness the courage to imagine a better world, one where equality isn't just an aspiration but a lived reality. This vision is forged from their deepest wishes and greatest frustrations, amalgamating into a powerful force for transformation.

These dream makers often draw strength from the past. By acknowledging the failures and triumphs of previous generations, they craft a roadmap that balances caution with courage. Historical victories serve as beacons, while past mistakes offer valuable lessons. This holistic perspective enables them to strategically navigate the nuances of societal change, ensuring that each step forward is both deliberate and impactful.

Visionaries are not just trailblazers; they are also wisdom keepers. Recognizing the value of intergenerational learning, they focus on preserving and passing down critical knowledge. They understand that the wisdom of our ancestors is a treasure trove of insights, guiding us to a more equitable future. By embracing and integrating this ancestral wisdom, they forge a cohesive narrative that connects past, present, and future into a tapestry of empowerment.

As visionaries of tomorrow, these remarkable women inspire us all to reclaim our autonomy over body, mind, heart, and spirit. They ignite fires of possibility, showing that true liberation comes from within and radiates outward. Let us follow their lead, celebrate their courage, and commit to a future where every woman can stand tall as a dream maker and wisdom keeper.

Using Yesterday's Failures and Victories to Shape Tomorrow's Dream

Recognizing that every misstep and triumph holds valuable lessons is how to use the failures and victories to bring wisdom for our walk tomorrow. When we draw from our collective history, we realize the power accumulated through each setback and success. Each loss teaches us resilience, and every victory provides a roadmap for future endeavors. By understanding the past, we forge a path toward a brighter, more equitable future.

Failures are not the end of the road but stepping stones toward growth. They challenge us to examine what went wrong, learn from our errors, and come back stronger and wiser. Each failure is a lesson in disguise, an opportunity to refine our strategies and approaches. Think about the countless women who have faced stumbling blocks in their journeys, only to rise again with renewed determination. The strength gathered from these moments is an arsenal that fortifies our resolve.

Similarly, our victories shape the landscape of our dreams. Successes, big or small, signify that progress is possible, that change is within our grasp. They are beacons of hope and affirmations of our capabilities. Victories serve as blueprints, showing us what works and inspiring confidence in our power to incite change. By celebrating these wins, we acknowledge our potential and motivate ourselves and others to persist in the pursuit of our dreams.

Reflect on the women's suffrage movement, a monumental triumph that took decades of tireless effort. These women faced numerous defeats, yet each one galvanized their resolve. Their ultimate victory wasn't just a political win; it was a testament to the power of perseverance and collective action. Their story isn't just history—it's a guidepost for us today. We stand on the shoulders of giants, and their achievements remind us that while the fight may be long, the rewards are profound.

Our dreams for tomorrow must be informed by the struggles and achievements of yesterday. These stories provide context and clarity, demonstrating that change is a continuous process. They also evoke the evolving nature of our challenges and opportunities. Patriarchy and oppression may take new forms, but the lessons learned from past engagements remain pertinent. We're equipped with a historical map, showing both the pitfalls and roads to success.

It's essential to document and share these stories to empower future generations. By preserving the tales of our ancestors and contemporaries, we curate a repository of wisdom for those who follow us. Each narrative is a piece of the larger mosaic of our collective journey towards liberation. When we pass down these lessons, we not only honor those who came before us but also arm the next generation with the knowledge and strength needed to continue the fight for equality and autonomy.

In crafting tomorrow's dreams, we must remember the struggles and victories that have shaped us. Our ancestors' dreams were deferred so that we could aspire higher. Acknowledging their sacrifices means committing to pushing our dreams, knowing they are achievable with tenacity and unity. Every setback we face isn't a dead-end but a valuable lesson that serves our ultimate purpose. Each success isn't the culmination of our efforts but a milestone in our journey towards a just and equitable world.

So, let's pledge to use the rich tapestry of our past to weave the fabric of our future. By doing so, we honor our history while creating a legacy of strength and resilience for those who will walk this path after us. Together, we can shape a world where dreams are not just imagined but realized.

Preserving and Passing Down Wisdom

Preserving and passing down wisdom is an act of love and survival, a lifeline connecting us to our ancestors and future generations. Wisdom isn't just knowledge; it is lived experience, molded by trials, triumphs, and timeless truths. For women, especially in a world often governed by patriarchal values, our wisdom holds the power to challenge, change, and heal.

Imagine wisdom as a meticulously woven tapestry, each thread a lesson, a piece of advice, a story of resilience. It doesn't just hang on the walls of antiquity; it is vibrant and alive, threaded through our daily lives, our decisions, and our dreams. This tapestry is an inheritance that all of us can contribute to, ensuring that it grows richer and more inclusive with each generation.

One vital aspect of preserving wisdom is our ability to share and communicate it effectively. In our stories and communal gatherings, be it around kitchen tables or digital platforms, we keep the wisdom alive. These stories are seeds planted in the hearts and minds of younger women, encouraging them to blossom into their strengths. It's through the sharing of these narratives that we arm them with the tools to navigate their own pathways, fortified with the courage and insights of those who came before.

Moreover, wisdom insists on an active practice of reflection and conscious living. By honoring our history and fully acknowledging the lessons from our past, we empower ourselves to make informed decisions for the future. This reflection demands that we look at both the successes and the painful experiences with equal rigor. Only then can we extract the pearls of wisdom that can guide us and the generations to come.

Passing down wisdom isn't just about words; it is about action and embodiment. When we model the principles we cherish—like integrity, compassion, resilience, and a steadfast commitment to justice—we give permission for others to do the same. Through our actions, we signify that the wisdom we preach is not an abstract concept but a lived reality, a source of enduring strength and hope.

Lastly, in preserving wisdom, we must be intentional about whom we uplift and learn from. Embracing diverse voices and experiences ensures that our collective wisdom grows more inclusive and representative of all women's lived realities. This continuous enrichment of wisdom is what will drive the transformative change we seek, establishing a foundation where the dreams of tomorrow's visionaries can be built securely on timeless truths.

Embracing Our Ancestral Wisdom for the Next Generation

How often do we find ourselves at a crossroads, seeking guidance to navigate our challenges? Our ancestors walked paths of resilience, wisdom, and unwavering spirit, leaving behind a treasure trove of knowledge. They may not have had modern tools, but their insights and experiences are invaluable for our journey today. It's time to embrace their legacy and pass it forward to the next generation.

Our ancestors understood the essence of community and connection, something that technology seems to eclipse in today's fast-paced world. They fostered environments where wisdom was shared in circles, under starry skies, and around the hearth. When we look to their practices, we discover that the power of storytelling, rituals, and traditions formed robust frameworks for understanding our place in the world. Let's reclaim these old ways to teach young girls and women about their intrinsic worth and potential for greatness.

Imagine what the world could look like if we intentionally integrate ancestral wisdom into our daily lives. Picture girls and young women being mentored in the art of listening to their inner voice, recognizing the cycles of nature, and honoring their bodies. Our foremothers knew the significance of these teachings, and they knew how to transfer this knowledge across generations. This isn't just about looking back; it's about moving forward with a fuller sense of who we are.

Another crucial aspect is the balance of self and community. Ancestral wisdom emphasized harmony within oneself and one's surroundings. For the next generation, teaching this balance means fostering a holistic understanding of life—one that blends mental, physical, emotional, and spiritual well-being. When young women grasp this interconnectedness, they cultivate a stronger sense of agency and purpose.

Moreover, we must not forget the resilience that our ancestors demonstrated. They faced oppression, displacement, and countless adversities, yet they rose, time and again, fortified by a deep-rooted wisdom. Today's struggles may appear different, but the lessons of resilience remain pertinent. Let's equip the next generation with these timeless tools to navigate their contemporary challenges with grace and strength.

Preserving ancestral wisdom also lies in honoring the land and nature. Our foremothers had a profound respect for Mother Earth and lived in reverence of her gifts. They understood the cycles of life and death, the importance of seasons, and the balance of give-and-take. Teaching our young women to reconnect with nature, to value sustainability and harmony, ensures that these critical lessons endure.

By passing down these teachings, we empower the next generation with a rich heritage that fuels their autonomy and sense of self. It's an educational journey that goes beyond textbooks, enriching them with the knowledge that they are part of something far more significant. Ancestral wisdom is a bridge to a stronger, more self-assured future, grounded in history yet ever forward-reaching.

So, let's actively create spaces where ancestral wisdom can flourish once more. We're not just preserving history; we're weaving it into the fabric of tomorrow's world. By doing so, we honor our past, invigorate our present, and build a transformative future that stands on the shoulders of giants. The next generation doesn't merely deserve this wisdom—they need it to thrive.

CHAPTER 9:
PRINCIPLES OF A SOVEREIGN SISTERHOOD

The journey toward a sovereign sisterhood is a profound reclamation of our sanctity, unity, and shared power. To be sovereign is to recognize that each woman's life is intrinsically valuable and interconnected with the lives of all other women, with a collective strength broader and deeper than the individual struggles we face. This understanding is the bedrock of our unity and equality. As we look around, we must see not competitors or adversaries, but sisters bound by the sacred mission to uplift and empower one another.

Unity doesn't mean uniformity. The beauty of a sisterhood lies in its diversity, the harmony of different voices, cultures, and experiences coming together. Each of us carries unique wisdom and has walked distinct paths. Recognizing and embracing these differences without judgment brings us closer to the heart of our collective divinity. We honor not only our individual journeys but also the sacred connection we share with our Earth Mother, whose nurturing spirit and strength we mirror and embody.

Central to the principles of a sovereign sisterhood is the concept of radical respect. This respect acknowledges our individual stories, our victories, and our scars. It champions the idea that each woman's experience, regardless of how it aligns with our own, holds a sacred value. We don't just stand alongside one another; we hold space, lift each other up, and create a tapestry of support that is unbreakable.

It is also essential to recognize the role of our shared spirituality. Our connection with the Earth, with the divine spirit within each of us, and with each other forms a triad of power that's unstoppable. Embracing this trinity brings a deeper understanding of ourselves and a stronger commitment to our shared journey.

As we strive to live out these principles daily, we acknowledge that the path to a sovereign sisterhood is ongoing. It requires us to be vigilant, compassionate, and steadfast. Truly embracing these principles means seeing every woman's struggle and triumph as our own, fostering an environment where every sister feels valued, seen, and heard.

In embracing these principles, we forge a community where the sanctity of our sisterhood is upheld by our collective actions and unwavering dedication. This sacred bond is our foundation for not just survival, but for thriving in a world that desperately needs our wisdom and strength.

Equality and Unity of Every Woman's Life

The very essence of a Sovereign Sisterhood begins with the unwavering commitment to the equality and unity of every woman's life. When we talk about equality, it's not just about ensuring equal opportunities or rights under the law. It extends to recognizing and valuing the unique experiences, strengths, and contributions of every woman, irrespective of her background, race, or socioeconomic status. This unity calls for us to uplift one another, breaking down the walls that historically have divided us.

Standing together in unity does not mean suppressing our individuality or uniqueness. On the contrary, it thrives on the celebration of our diverse identities. Our diversity is our strength, not a barrier. By understanding and honoring our differences, we enrich the sisterhood, nurturing a space where every woman feels seen, heard, and valued.

Reclaiming our autonomy over body, mind, heart, and spirit starts with the recognition of our inherent worth. Patriarchal systems have long thrived on making women believe they are lesser, fragmented, and powerless. To transcend this, we must reclaim the narrative of our lives. This journey comes from within, by internalizing that every woman—every sister—has an equal stake in the shared vision of liberation and empowerment. It's not a solitary journey but a collective one, where each step forward is a victory for all.

Unity is not a passive state. It's an active, ongoing commitment. It requires us to listen deeply, to empathize, and to advocate for one another. This means challenging our biases, addressing injustices we witness, and standing up when a sister is being oppressed. It's not enough to avoid harm; we must also act as allies and advocates, creating safe spaces where healing and growth are possible.

Our unity is inextricably linked to our individual freedoms. As long as any woman is oppressed, none of us are truly free. Liberation is a collective effort and our unity is its core. We must understand that our liberation is bound together; our strength is in our togetherness. When we support each other's journeys towards self-discovery and empowerment, we cultivate a sisterhood that's resilient and unstoppable.

The principles of equality and unity demand that we speak up for those who can't find their voice and amplify the voices that are often silenced. This unity isn't built solely on agreements and similarities, but on the respect for the richness of our experiences. By weaving together our narratives of struggle, resilience, and triumph, we build a tapestry that's vibrant, strong, and unbreakable.

This sisterhood transcends borders and generations. It's about passing down the wisdom of past struggles and weaving it into the fabric of future victories. This connection through time and space forms a continuum of solidarity, where each woman's story adds a thread to the larger narrative of our collective empowerment.

In the end, our unity and equality are not just ideals but living principles that guide our actions and interactions. They remind us that we are stronger together, and that our combined strength can dismantle the patriarchal structures that seek to divide and diminish us. Together, we forge a path where every woman's life is valued and her potential is limitless. Each of us holds a piece of the collective power needed to transform not just our lives, but the world.

Embracing the Divinity of One Another and Our Earth Mother

As we walk this journey of reclaiming our innate sovereignty, it's paramount to recognize the divinity within ourselves and each other. When we honor the sacredness of our sisterhood, we build a resilient fabric woven from threads of compassion, strength, and mutual respect. This chapter encourages us to see beyond the superficial aspects of our interactions and delve into the core essence of our shared humanity. Here we begin to dismantle the harmful paradigms that have long kept us separated and disempowered.

Recognizing the divinity in one another means acknowledging that every woman carries a piece of the divine within her. It's a powerful affirmation of our connectedness and worth. When we see our sisters through this lens, the nuances of jealousy, competition, and distrust fade away, replaced by a deeper commitment to support and uplift each other. This perspective shift isn't just spiritual rhetoric; it's a foundational principle that has practical implications in our everyday lives. It encourages us to foster environments where respect and unity are paramount.

Our relationship with the Earth Mother is equally crucial. The Earth is not merely a resource to be exploited; she is alive, breathing, and nurturing. She sustains us, and in return, it's our sacred duty to honor and protect her. By embracing this symbiotic relationship, we begin to see environmental stewardship not as an obligation, but as a privilege and a form of worship. As we heal the Earth, we heal ourselves.

Imagine a world where our collective actions are rooted in the reverence for all living beings. This shift in consciousness requires us to adopt practices that promote sustainability and harmony. Simple acts, such as reducing waste, supporting eco-friendly products, and advocating for environmental justice, become acts of love. They strengthen our bond with the Earth and each other. When we see the Earth as a divine entity, our actions towards her shift from exploitation to nurturing, from indifference to deep care.

In our sisterhood, embracing divinity calls us to celebrate our diversity, rather than use it as a tool of division. The richness of our varied experiences, histories, and cultural backgrounds is what makes our collective so powerful. Instead of allowing patriarchal structures to dictate our worth based on conformity, we stand tall in our unique identities and encourage our sisters to do the same. This mutual recognition fuels the fires of change and empowers us to challenge the very systems that seek to oppress us.

To foster this ethos, we must actively engage in practices that nurture our spiritual and emotional well-being. This might include rituals, meditation, or simply spending time in nature, listening to the whispers of the wind and the songs of the birds. These moments of connection ground us, remind us of our place in the greater tapestry of life, and fortify us for the work ahead.

As we look inward and outward, let's maintain a balanced perspective. Internal healing and self-care are vital, but equally important is our responsibility to our community and the Earth. By nurturing a holistic approach, we recognize that our well-being is intricately tied to that of our sisters and our environment. This interconnectedness is the bedrock of a sovereign sisterhood, empowering us to act with integrity and love.

In conclusion, embracing the divinity of one another and our Earth Mother is not a distant ideal; it's a must lived reality that we can cultivate through intentional action and heartfelt connection. As we honor the sacred within and around us, we pave the way for a liberated future where all can thrive. Our journey is not just about reclaiming autonomy but about recognizing and nurturing the inherent sacredness in every breath, every step, and every interaction.

CHAPTER 10:
EMPOWERING THE NEXT GENERATION

Teaching sovereign principles to the next generation is perhaps the most powerful act of mentorship we can offer. Imagine a world where young women grow up knowing their worth—not as prescribed by society but as determined by their own innate power and wisdom. This is not merely a utopian vision but a practical pathway to sustainable change. By instilling principles of self-determination, bodily autonomy, and emotional resilience, we unleash a generation equipped to dismantle outdated norms and redefine what it means to thrive.

Nurturing tomorrow's leaders demands more than just lip service. It calls for active engagement, mentorship, and genuinely listening to their voices. Our role isn't to dictate their paths but to provide the tools and space necessary for them to discover and own their power. Empowerment is a two-way street. As we guide, we also learn. Young people offer fresh perspectives, reminding us of the importance of adaptability and innovation. Let us not forget, true leadership lies in inspiring others to believe in their abilities.

To foster this environment, we must cultivate communities that encourage curiosity and celebrate failure as an integral part of growth. Safe spaces where young women feel valued and understood spur creativity and bold action. When they see their mentors—us—taking risks, owning our stories, and challenging systemic barriers, it ignites a spark within them to do the same. They begin to understand that their dreams are valid, their voices are essential, and that they are not alone in their journey.

As we embrace our roles as mentors and guides, let's remember that the wisdom we pass on today shapes the leaders of tomorrow. We owe it to future generations to show them, through our actions and words, the immeasurable power of unity, resilience, and self-sovereignty. When one of us rises, we all rise. And in this collective ascent, we are crafting a future where every woman—every individual—is free to flourish beyond the constraints of patriarchal expectations.

The legacy we leave for tomorrow starts with what we do today. Let's empower the next generation to not just inherit the world, but to transform it.

Teaching Sovereign Principles

Understanding and embracing sovereign principles starts with the foundational belief that each of us has the right to full autonomy over our bodies, minds, hearts, and spirits. This belief is revolutionary in a world that often tries to undermine these rights through a matrix of oppressive systems. The next generation of women must learn to anchor themselves in this knowledge, fortifying their own sovereignty to effectively challenge and dismantle these systems.

Imagine a world where young women are educated not just in traditional academic subjects but in the truths of their own power and autonomy. Our task is to inspire this vision into reality by introducing sovereign principles in education systems, community programs, and family teachings. This means exposing young minds to the evidence of their inherent worth and capability and shielding them from societal messages that diminish their potential.

Teaching sovereign principles involves a multifaceted approach. It's not just about individual empowerment but also creating environments that support and nurture this growth. When we educate girls about their rights to their own bodies, thoughts, and feelings, we're planting seeds of resilience and independence. These teachings can unfold through shared stories of triumph over adversity, lessons in emotional intelligence, and practices that encourage self-reflection and inner strength.

A crucial aspect of this educational journey is emphasizing the importance of community and sisterhood. Sovereignty doesn't mean isolation; it means standing tall in your autonomy while recognizing and upholding the sovereignty of others. This interconnection is vital. When each woman knows and feels her own power, the collective becomes an unbreakable force capable of creating real, lasting change.

Our focus must also be on addressing and deconstructing internalized patriarchy. Many young women grow up internalizing societal expectations and gender norms that limit their understanding of their own potential. Teaching sovereign principles involves making them aware of these societal impositions, helping them see their true selves beyond societal constructs, and empowering them to reject what doesn't serve their growth and well-being.

Encouraging young women to question, challenge, and redefine what power and success mean to them is transformative. This creates a new paradigm where they feel confident to pursue their aspirations, contribute meaningfully to society, and support one another. By instilling these values, we prepare the next generation not just to survive but to thrive and become catalysts for widespread transformation.

As mentors, leaders, and role models, we have a duty to model these principles. Our actions, words, and approaches must reflect the sovereignty we seek to instill in the younger generation. This is not a one-time lesson but an ongoing process of engagement, reflection, and affirmation. By being unwavering in our commitment to teaching and embodying these sovereign principles, we pave the way for a future where every woman can confidently own her power and place in the world.

In essence, teaching sovereign principles is about offering the next generation the tools and knowledge they need to reclaim their autonomy and liberate themselves from oppressive structures. This empowers them to become the fearless leaders of tomorrow, capable of creating a more just and equitable world. By fostering an environment that celebrates and supports their sovereignty, we can indeed transform the world, one empowered woman at a time.

Nurturing Tomorrow's Leaders

Nurturing tomorrow's leaders is not just a responsibility, it's an act of love and trust in the future. We're at a pivotal moment where the next generation of women and those identifying as female can redefine leadership. This chapter serves as a compass, guiding us on how to cultivate empowered leaders who will challenge and transform societal norms.

Inspiring leadership in young women starts with teaching them to value themselves. When they see their worth, they start to believe in their ability to effect change. We must encourage them to voice their ideas, no matter how unconventional they might seem. This cultivation of self-worth is the fertile ground from which confident leaders grow.

Role models play a crucial role in nurturing tomorrow's leaders. We need real, relatable examples of empowerment. Young women should see leaders who understand the struggles and the triumphs of being female in a patriarchal society. When they can identify with these role models, they gain the strength to envision themselves in leadership roles.

However, providing role models is just part of the equation. We must also offer opportunities for young women to practice leadership. It means giving them platforms to speak, spaces to organize, and the resources to initiate change. Experiencing leadership first-hand molds them into adept and adaptable leaders.

This nurturing process also involves teaching critical thinking and emotional intelligence. Future leaders must learn to question existing paradigms and think independently. They should also develop the empathy and compassion needed to lead with heart. Leadership is not just about decisions; it's about understanding the human impact of those decisions.

It's essential to create environments where young women feel safe to express themselves without fear of judgment or reprisal. Safe spaces cultivate the confidence to explore new ideas and take risks. These environments should encourage collaboration rather than competition, allowing young leaders to support and learn from each other.

Encouraging activism in areas they are passionate about is another way to nurture future leaders. This activism can take many forms, from local community work to global movements. The important thing is to help them find their voice in the context of something that matters deeply to them. Activism empowers them to see the impact they can have.

A key component of nurturing leadership is teaching the importance of resilience. The ability to bounce back from setbacks is crucial for any leader. Show them that failure is not the end but a stepping stone to greater growth. Resilience builds perseverance, a quality that will carry them through the inevitable challenges of leadership.

Let's also not forget the power of storytelling. Sharing stories of women who have overcome obstacles to lead can inspire and motivate. These stories should include diverse voices from different backgrounds and paths to leadership. They provide a rich tapestry of experiences from which young women can draw strength and inspiration.

In conclusion, nurturing tomorrow's leaders requires a multifaceted approach. We must combine self-worth, role models, opportunities, critical thinking, emotional intelligence, safe spaces, activism, resilience, and storytelling. By doing so, we lay the groundwork for a new generation of empowered, compassionate, and visionary leaders who can break barriers and build a more inclusive world.

CHAPTER 11:
INSPIRING ACTION

Inspiration without action is like a vessel with no wind; it remains still and stagnant. We've journeyed through understanding the depths of our oppression, celebrated our inner strength, and healed old wounds. Now it's time to move forward, to channel all this empowered energy into tangible change. This isn't just about individual transformations but about igniting collective efforts that create ripples of change across our communities and beyond.

Mobilizing for change *now* has never been more crucial. It's in our hands to dismantle the systems of oppression that have long held us back. Whether it's through grassroots movements, policy advocacy, or community organizing, every effort counts. Start small if you must— perhaps by gathering like-minded women in your neighborhood to discuss local issues and brainstorm solutions. Small circles often evolve into powerful movements when fueled by shared purpose and passion.

Consider the collective power we're capable of wielding. Think of it as a tapestry being woven with countless threads, each unique yet bound together by a common goal. We must strive to include diverse voices in our efforts, ensuring that every woman, regardless of her background, feels seen, heard, and valued. Diversity isn't just about representation; it's about enriching our struggle with multiple perspectives that make our movements more robust and inclusive.

Our role doesn't end with mobilization; it extends to sustaining this momentum. This requires perseverance and resilience. Communicate consistently, support one another, and hold space for rest and rejuvenation—our energy is not inexhaustible, and neither should it be. Sustainable action is about finding balance and ensuring that our drive for change doesn't deplete our well-being.

The time for waiting is over. We've done the healing, the understanding, and the growing. Every step you've taken so far has prepared you for this moment—to act, to lead, and to inspire others to join you in creating the world we envision. Let's channel our collective wisdom and unwavering spirit to inspire actions that liberate and uplift us all.

Mobilizing for Change NOW

Our current reality is a testament to the incredible potential we have when we come together, mobilize, and create meaningful change. It's high time we harness the collective power of every woman and those who identify as female, rising as a united front against oppression. This isn't about waiting for the perfect moment or the right set of circumstances. It's about taking action now, with the tools, knowledge, and passion that we already possess.

Every great movement in history started with individuals who dared to dream and acted on their visions. It's no different today. To mobilize for change now, we must first believe unequivocally in our capability to influence the world. Our voices are potent, our hearts are resilient, and our spirits are unbreakable. Each of us holds within us a spark needed to ignite the fires of transformation.

Consider the power of grassroots mobilization. From organizing local community groups to leveraging the far-reaching influence of social media, every effort counts. Local actions catalyze global reactions, creating ripples of change that thunder across continents. Start small if need be: host a discussion group, attend a rally, write an op-ed, or mentor young women in your community. Every action, no matter how seemingly insignificant, contributes to the greater cause.

Collaboration is essential. Aligning ourselves with like-minded individuals and organizations amplifies our voices. When we pool our resources, experiences, and wisdom, we build a formidable front that's hard to ignore. Unity does not mean uniformity; it means embracing our diverse strengths and backgrounds to work towards a common goal. The richer our tapestry of support, the stronger we become.

Mobilizing now also requires a willingness to confront uncomfortable truths. We must honestly assess the areas where we've been complacent or complicit in upholding patriarchal structures. This introspection is vital. By acknowledging these aspects, we can dismantle them within ourselves, which, in turn, emboldens us to confront them in societal norms and institutions. Our liberation starts from within, but its resonance is profoundly external.

Moreover, it's crucial to stay informed and educated. To mobilize effectively, we need to understand the landscape of the issues we're tackling. Engaging with historical contexts, current events, and policy changes helps ground our efforts in reality and strategize adequately. Whether it's attending workshops, reading crucial literature, or staying updated on legislative developments, knowledge equips us to navigate resistance with grace and grit.

Perhaps most importantly, we must cultivate resilience. Mobilizing for change is a marathon filled with bouts of frustration, setbacks, and obstacles. Yet it's in these challenges that our true power shines. Every step forward, no matter how fraught with difficulties, is a testament to our resolve and courage. The strength of a movement is measured not just by its successes but by its capacity to endure and thrive through adversity.

Let's also honor the small victories. Change often comes incrementally. Celebrate the milestones, no matter how minor they may seem. These moments of triumph fuel our drive and remind us that progress is possible. They keep the flame of hope alive, inspiring others to join and sustain the momentum.

In mobilizing for change now, we're not just advocating for ourselves but for future generations. Our actions today lay the groundwork for a more equitable and just world where every girl, woman, and non-binary individual can thrive. The time for introspection is over; the era of decisive action is upon us.

So, let's move forward with determination, passion, and unwavering belief in our collective power. Together, we can transform our dreams of liberation into reality. Let's start now.

Collective Efforts and Movements

The power to enact change lies in unity—the joining of hearts, minds, and spirits toward a common goal. Throughout history, collective efforts and movements have been the cornerstone of women's advanceement and the betterment of society. Consider the numerous suffrage movements worldwide; their unyielding determination achieved the monumental milestone of women's right to vote. These endeavors show that when women band together, the impossible becomes possible.

Movements, whether big or small, spark revolutions in society. Take, for example, the #MeToo movement, which began as individual stories of pain and resilience shared online. This movement grew into a global phenomenon, leading to real-world consequences for perpetrators of abuse and profound changes in workplace policies. Today, the resistance movement toward the patriarchy is for bodily autonomy. This is the face, voice and action of our collective empowerment, our sovereign sisterhood. It's a testament to the idea that our voices, once united, resonate louder and further than we could ever imagine.

Social media has transformed the landscape of activism, making it easier for women across the globe to connect and mobilize. Platforms like Twitter, Instagram, and Facebook offer instant communication and organization. Online petitions, virtual protests, and awareness campaigns can gain traction at lightning speed. This digital revolution enables us not just to react to injustice but to proactively seek out areas that need change and address them head-on.

Historically, women's movements have often intersected with other social justice causes, forming a broader coalition for change. The struggle for racial, economic, and environmental justice has frequently found allies in the women's movement. This intersectionality enriches our collective efforts, bringing diverse perspectives and strengths to the table. It's a reminder that our fight is not isolated; it is part of a larger, interconnected struggle for a just world.

Solidarity is more than just a concept—it is an active practice. In communities where women support each other, we see exponential growth in courage, innovation, and success. Programs that offer mentorship, community support, and shared resources enable women to break free from cycles of abuse and deprivation. These grassroots initiatives can become national movements, influencing policy and reshaping societal norms.

Engaging in collective movements also involves understanding the power dynamics at play. It's crucial to confront internalized patriarchy and dismantle it from within our groups. A conscious effort to ensure inclusivity and equality within these movements broadens their impact. By respecting and valuing every voice, we build stronger alliances and fortify our resolve against the external forces of oppression.

Organizing and mobilizing for change can be daunting, but efforts are rewarded with resilience and transformation. Every moment dedicated to planning, rallying, and advocating counts. Whether through traditional methods like marches and rallies or newer strategies such as viral social media campaigns, the cumulative effect of our actions drives societal evolution.

Volunteering and engaging with local and global organizations also amplify our impact. From participating in community service projects to lobbying for legislative changes, every effort contributes to the seismic shifts needed to dismantle systemic inequalities.

Remember that collective efforts and movements are not relinquished to the pages of history; they are living phenomena shaped by our current actions. Your participation carries the torch of countless women who fought before you and ignites the flame of those who will carry it forward. When we unite our voices and our will, we become an unstoppable force for change. Through solidarity and action, we can inspire a world where every woman, everywhere, reclaims her autonomy and her power.

CONCLUSION

We've traversed a profound journey together—one that unravels the threads of patriarchal dominance and reweaves them into a tapestry of empowerment. This book couldn't strip away centuries of oppression in a few pages, but it aimed to ignite your spirit, to light the pathway for your autonomy. Every story, every struggle, is a testament to the indomitable power that lies within you.

It's crucial to remember that reclaiming your body, mind, heart, and spirit is not a linear path but a cyclical process of owning, transforming, and healing. You are not the sum of your traumas; instead, you are the phoenix rising from the ashes, gathering strength from each trial. Carry this understanding with you: your power is both inherent and infinite.

Moreover, our bonds of sisterhood are where revolutions begin. By healing the wounds inflicted by internalized patriarchy, we build an unbreakable network of support. We're stronger together, capable of fostering change that not only benefits us but also uplifts those around us. Through compassionate understanding and heart-centered leadership, we become the WayShowers and TruthTellers the world desperately needs.

As custodians of immense wisdom and visionaries of a better tomorrow, it's essential to pass down what we've learned to the next generation. Teach them the principles of sovereignty and unity, nurture their potential, and inspire them to be the dream makers of the future. It is through these actions that we sustain the momentum of this movement.

In closing, let this book be both a mirror and a window. A mirror to reflect your boundless possibilities, and a window to the collective change we are capable of creating. Mobilize for change now. Your individual efforts contribute to a larger, collective movement. Together, we will dismantle the systems that have long oppressed us and forge a new world where every woman can stand in her full power. The time for action is now; the future is ours to shape.

Appendix A: Resources

As you embark on your journey towards reclaiming your autonomy and strengthening your spirit, mind, and body, having a robust set of resources is crucial. Knowledge empowers us, and unity solidifies our strengths; with every resource, we gain tools and allies for the path ahead. Below, you'll find some suggested books, websites, and workshops/retreats that will help you get started; stay supported, as you navigate this transformative process.

Books

- **"Women Who Run With the Wolves" by Clarissa Pinkola Estés**: This groundbreaking book delves into the stories and myths that shape women's instincts and creativity.

- **"Untamed" by Glennon Doyle**: Doyle's powerful memoir encourages women to trust themselves and live free from societal constraints.

- **"The Beauty Myth" by Naomi Wolf**: An exploration of how beauty standards oppress women, offering a critical look at body image and cultural pressures.

- Other titles & Authors: "Uncomfortable Labels: My Life as a Gay, Autistic, Trans Woman" by Laura Kate Dale; "Revolution From Within: A Book of Self-Esteem" by Gloria Steinem; "Yoke: My Yoga of Self-Acceptance" by Jessamyn Stanley; "I Am Malala" by Malala Yousefzai & Christina Lamb; "The Source of Self-Regard" by Toni Morrison; "In the Company of Women" by Grace Bouney; "Year of the Tiger: An Activist Life" by Alice Wong; "We Should All Be Feminists" by Chimamanda Ngozi Adichie; "Long After We Are Gone" by Terah Shelton Harris; "Woman, Race & Class" by Angela G. Davis; "Nasty Women: Feminism, Resistance & Revolution in Trump's America" by Samhita Mukhopadhyay; "Why You Matter" by Eli PaintedCrow

Websites

- *BUST* (www.bust.com): This online platform features articles and resources that focus on feminist perspectives, culture, and lifestyle.

- *The Representation Project*

  (www.therepresentationproject.org): Advocating for the eradication of gender stereotypes, this project provides various resources for activism and education.

- *Everyday Feminism* (www.everydayfeminism.com): This site offers insightful articles, online courses, and webinars to help readers understand and challenge societal oppression.

Workshops and Retreats

- *Omega Institute for Holistic Studies* (www.eomega.org):

  Offering a wide array of workshops and retreats focusing on women's empowerment, healing arts, and personal growth.

- *Esalen Institute* (www.esalen.org):

  Located in Big Sur, California, Esalen provides transformational workshops which include those specifically aimed at reclaiming female strength and spirit.

- ***Kripalu Center for Yoga & Health***

  (www.kripalu.org): This center offers numerous retreats and programs that focus on spiritual and emotional growth, with specific events designed to support women's journeys.

These resources are here to support you as you make choices to own all facets of yourself joyfully and powerfully. Dive into these books for inspiration and understanding, explore websites for guidance and community, and consider workshops or retreats to deepen your transformation. Together, we rise, holding each other up as we reclaim what has always been ours—our sovereignty and our strength.

Books

Diving into the wealth of written wisdom can be a transformative experience for any woman seeking to reclaim her autonomy and ignite change. Books have always been a gateway to knowledge, providing us with the insights and tools necessary to navigate the complexities of life. Here, we'll focus on literature that not only empowers but also challenges the patriarchal narratives that have long dictated the lives of women.

Consider reading works that explore themes of female sovereignty, resilience, and healing. These books offer valuable perspectives on overcoming oppression and embracing one's true self. They serve as both guides and companions on the journey to self-liberation.

Some essential reads cover the historical struggles and triumphs of women worldwide, offering lessons from past resistance movements. They highlight the strength and wisdom gained from our foremothers' battles and show how those lessons are still relevant today.

Think about works that delve into the intricacies of trauma and transformation. These books often provide personal narratives and professional insights that can help you understand and harness your own experiences of pain and resilience. By reading about others' journeys, we find parallels to our own, learning how to transform trauma into a source of power and purpose.

There are also books that address internalized patriarchy and the importance of sisterhood. These works are particularly powerful as they help us uncover the subtle ways we may have absorbed patriarchal values and offer strategies to heal and strengthen our bonds with other women. By fostering a supportive and unified sisterhood, we become more capable of enacting meaningful change.

Lastly, the literature that focuses on visionaries and wisdom keepers will inspire you with stories of heart-centered leadership and the preservation of ancestral knowledge. These books remind us of the importance of embracing our heritage and carrying forward the wisdom of our ancestors, ensuring a brighter future for the next generations.

In summary, the right books can serve as powerful allies in your journey towards empowerment and self-discovery. They are filled with the stories and strategies of those who have walked the path before us, offering guidance and solidarity. Keep an open heart and mind, and let these written works be your stepping stones to a more liberated you.

Websites

- BUST (www.bust.com): This online platform features articles and resources that focus on feminist perspectives, culture, and lifestyle.

- The Representation Project (www.therepresentation-project.org): Advocating for the eradication of gender stereotypes, this project provides various resources for activism and education.

- Everyday Feminism (www.everydayfeminism.com): This site offers insightful articles, online courses, and webinars to help readers understand and challenge societal oppression.

Turtle Women Rising supporting global female sovereignty within and among us toward a world transformation of peace, harmony and compassion where we all can thrive (www.turtlewomenrising-live.com): this site is embarking on a campaign of solidarity and unity of voice: "VOTE for a Path of Sovereignty" that can be used in political campaigns around the world where women's autonomy is at stake. This campaign will be followed with an international call to "Choose a Path of Sovereignty"

In the digital age, knowledge and community can be found at our fingertips. Websites dedicated to the empowerment and advancement of gender female across the globe are pivotal in our collective journey toward sovereignty. They are hubs of information, inspiration, and connection, where we can learn from each other's experiences, share our triumphs, and mobilize for change.

One of the most powerful aspects of these online platforms is their ability to unite us across distances. Whether you're looking for historical resources, forums for discussion, or organizations actively fighting against patriarchal structures, there's a wealth of websites that can guide and support you in reclaiming your autonomy.

Websites like *Everyday Feminism* offer a multitude of articles addressing various aspects of daily life and the systemic challenges we face. Their pieces aim to educate and empower, providing practical advice and perspectives that challenge the status quo. Similarly, platforms like *Ms. Magazine* and *Bitch Media* delve into feminist discourse, highlighting pressing issues and celebrating the achievements of women worldwide.

If you're seeking a community of like-minded individuals, websites such as *The Sisterhood* and *Lean In* offer spaces to connect with others who share your vision for equality and justice. These communities are invaluable for those looking to find support, share experiences, and strategize ways to effect change.

For those driven to action, websites like *Women Who Code* and *Girls Who Code* provide resources to break into tech, an industry historically dominated by men. Similarly, initiatives like *She Should Run* encourage women to take up leadership roles in government, equipping them with the tools and knowledge necessary for political careers.

In addition to community and activism resources, there are also educational sites such as *Coursera* and *edX*, which offer courses that can help you expand your knowledge and skills in areas critical to your personal and professional growth.

Ultimately, these websites are more than just digital pages; they are beacons of hope and reservoirs of collective strength. By engaging with them, you become part of a vast network of empowered women and those identifying as female, conscious change agents all committed to breaking free from patriarchal constraints and fostering a world where every voice is heard, and every life is valued.

Workshops and Retreats

Omega Institute for Holistic Studies (www.eomega.org): Offering a wide array of workshops and retreats focusing on women's empowerment, healing arts, and personal growth.

- Esalen Institute (www.esalen.org): Located in Big Sur, California, Esalen provides transformational workshops which include those specifically aimed at reclaiming female strength and spirit.

- Kripalu Center for Yoga & Health (www.kripalu.org): This center offers numerous retreats and programs that focus on spiritual and emotional growth, with specific events designed to support women's journeys.

These are some national and well-known workshops and retreats. Search locally for women's retreats that serve to support your own journeys of reclaiming power. Find ones that resonate with you, culturally. Find ones where the WayShowers live and demonstrate their own journeys of progress and change. Trust your intuition and heart for whatever feels right and for what you are ready for. These resources are here to support you as you make choices to own all facets of yourself joyfully and powerfully. Dive into these books for inspiration and understanding, explore websites for guidance and community, and consider workshops or retreats to deepen your transformation. Together, we rise, holding each other up as we reclaim what has always been ours—our sovereignty and our strength.

Workshops and retreats offer powerful avenues for transformation and empowerment. These immersive experiences are designed to cultivate a safe space where we can reconnect with our authentic selves, develop deeper bonds with our sisters, and reimagine what is possible for our lives and the world around us.

By participating in these gatherings, we step outside our daily routines and immerse ourselves in environments that foster growth, healing, and empowerment. Through carefully curated activities, guided reflections, and communal support, we tap into collective wisdom and individual strengths. These experiences challenge us to confront and dismantle the internalized patriarchal beliefs that often limit our potential.

Workshops often focus on a variety of topics that help nurture our body, mind, heart, and spirit. Whether it's through creative expression, mindfulness practices, physical movement, or deep dialogues, each workshop is an opportunity to explore different facets of our being. These settings encourage us to acknowledge our pain, celebrate our resilience, and transform our trauma into a force for positive change.

Retreats offer a more extended period for reflection and connection. In these sacred spaces, we have the chance to detox from the external pressures of society and dive deeply into self-discovery. Surrounded by nature or in a tranquil setting, retreats allow for intensive healing work, providing the solitude and support necessary to reclaim parts of ourselves that have been suppressed or neglected.

At both workshops and retreats, you will encounter like-minded women on similar journeys. The camaraderie and sisterhood that form in these spaces are invaluable. Sharing our stories and listening to those of others help us realize that we are not alone in our struggles. Together, we build a supportive network that transcends the retreat or workshop, offering ongoing encouragement and solidarity as we navigate our paths of empowerment.

The facilitators of these workshops and retreats are often experienced leaders who bring their unique blend of knowledge, compassion, and guidance. They create a nurturing environment where every participant feels seen, heard, and valued. Through their mentorship, we gain new tools and perspectives that equip us to face the challenges of living in a patriarchal society with renewed strength and clarity.

Investing time in workshops and retreats is a profound act of self-love and commitment to our personal growth. These spaces remind us of our inherent power and potential, encouraging us to take bold steps toward a future where our autonomy and sovereignty are fully realized. By embracing these opportunities, we not only transform ourselves but become catalysts for change in our communities and beyond.

Consider the upcoming workshops and retreats listed in the resources section as your next step toward reclaiming your power. Each one is a stepping stone on the journey to becoming the liberated, sovereign woman you are meant to be.

www.ingramcontent.com/pod-product-compliance
Lightning Source LLC
Chambersburg PA
CBHW030408290526
45785CB00004B/1937